Dear Ford and Alessa,
Thank you both for your support and friendship!
Rebecca

Conventional Wisdom

How Today's Leaders Plan, Perform, and Progress Like the Founding Fathers

Rebecca Staton-Reinstein, Ph.D.

© Rebecca Staton-Reinstein - Advantage Leadership, Inc.
Printed in the United States

All Rights Reserved. No part of this book may be reproduced in any form or by any means without prior written permission from the author or publisher except for brief quotations embodied in critical essays, articles, or reviews. These articles and/or reviews must state the correct title and contributing author of this book by name.

For additional copies contact:
Advantage Leadership, Inc.
Phone: (305) 652-3466
http://www.AdvantageLeadership.com

Published by:
TobsusPress
1835 NE Miami Gardens Dr., Suite 151
North Miami Beach, FL 33179

Publisher's Cataloging-in-Publication

   Staton-Reinstein, Rebecca.
     Conventional wisdom : how today's leaders plan,
   perform, and progress like the founding fathers /
   Rebecca Staton-Reinstein.
     p. cm.
     Includes bibliographical references and index.
     LCCN 2008934768
     ISBN-13: 978-0-9715578-3-3
     ISBN-10: 0-9715578-3-7

   1. Leadership. 2. Strategic planning.   I. Title.

HD57.7.S73 2008   658.4'092
                   QBI08-600238

This book is dedicated to my parents,
Ralph Staton and Ruth Necessary Jett Staton,
who taught me to love history.

Table of Contents

Author's Forward 1
How the "Mighty Little Madison" Saved My Life

Preamble 7

Article I 25
Deal With the Real

Article II 39
Bring Vision to Reality

Article III 69
Get People on a Mission

Article IV 83
The Road Re-Traveled

Article V 103
"Mistakes Were Made"

Article VI **135**
    Execution is Harder than Revolution

Article VII **165**
    Nurturing Human Nature

Amendments **189**
    Failure to Improve is Not an Option

Postscript **205**
    What is Strategic Leadership?

Chapter Notes **221**

Acknowledgements **237**

Bibliography **243**

Index **255**

Author's Foreword

How the "Mighty Little Madison"[1] Saved My Life (With a Little Help From a Friend)

The train hurtled up out of the tunnel into the crisp September air. Ordinarily, being in my home state of Virginia would give me a lift, a tiny thrill of familiarity. My parents were history lovers who brought the history of our state and country to life for me. My daddy and I had hiked, fished, and camped around the state, reveling in its natural beauty. But as I glanced out the window this particular morning, I couldn't avoid seeing the smoke still staining the sky as it rose from the decimated building we passed. I couldn't lift the feeling of doom and angst that had overtaken me just twenty-four hours before. I couldn't erase the televised pictures of planes hitting skyscrapers and debris strewn across a farmer's field in an endless loop of devastation. Now I stared out the window, not at a flickering picture, but at reality.

For many people in the aftermath of that horrible day, depression eventually lifted as we adjusted to the new world we were forced to inhabit. Yet over a year later, I hadn't bounced back. I still ate too much comfort food, didn't sleep well, and just couldn't find any joy.

I finally went to see a counselor, who diagnosed Post Traumatic Stress Disorder. For the next year or so, we worked together and slowly tried to strip away my demons. She suggested I focus more on my creative endeavors and start to read again. At first I was skeptical, but I was also desperate. I pulled together material I had been using with my clients and published a workbook on strategic planning and created some other information products.

At the same time, I started reading history again. I always depended on understanding the past to make sense of the present, especially in my beloved country. My daddy's idea of a vacation was tramping across old battlefields, picking up minié balls, climbing redoubts, and recreating famous battles before me with his vivid storytelling. Mama made sure we visited every historic home and site we could, and eased long car rides with tales of the exploits of historic figures.

When I followed her path by attending the College of William and Mary, I was enchanted by the eighteenth century and generally soaked up as much of that magical place as possible. I worked for the Colonial Williamsburg Foundation for two years, wearing period costumes and interpreting the past for people visiting the restored and reconstructed buildings.

Now, in trying to understand the present through the mirror of the past, I read the masterful new biographies of Alexander Hamilton and John Adams, then breaking sales records. I discovered Joseph Ellis' masterpieces and started devouring everything of his I could find. After all, he was also a graduate of William and Mary!

Discussions of the Constitutional Convention in almost every book led me to my own bookcase and Catherine Drinker Bowen's *Miracle in Philadelphia*. It was a special bicentennial edition I bought, but never read. I was soon awash in the debates and her fascinating day-by-day account of that astounding event.

One lazy Saturday afternoon, I was ensconced in our library, reading. I paid no heed to the lovely South Florida sunshine outside. Suddenly, I sat bolt upright. "No, it can't be," I said to myself. "This is just one of those passing thoughts — they seem very cool at the moment, but evaporate quickly under a little light scrutiny."

So I scrutinized. I kept reading, furiously now, trying to disprove my own hypothesis. I thought of the one person who might confirm or deny my musings, my former husband, Dick

Perles. He was a lawyer, and constitutional law had fascinated him since our school days at William and Mary. I shot off an e-mail with my premise and waited for a response.

I happened to look up at my bookshelf and spied a battered paperbound book among old textbooks on government. I took it down. The pages were cluttered with underlines and margin notes in a familiar hand. I looked at the flyleaf. Scrawled there was my former husband's name and his dorm room number. It was his copy of *The Federal Convention and the Formation of the Union of the American States*, with excerpts from James Madison's notes on our Constitutional Convention.

The book had been packed, unpacked, and repacked countless times since 1971 when my husband and I parted ways. I had never consciously looked at it. I had no idea why he left it behind. But there it was, and I couldn't put it down. I tore through the yellowed pages and yearned for more.

A few days later, I got a reply to my e-mail, and it was a crushing blow.

You see, my shaky idea was this: what those men did in Philadelphia over two hundred years ago was hammer out a strategic plan for the new United States that would be embodied in the new Constitution. The framers of the Constitution were using the same techniques contemporary leaders use to develop strategic plans for their organizations.

After praising my effort and offering a few insights and suggestions for reading, Dick concluded, "The constitutional convention was not a model of strategic planning, but rather a messy affair."

I fumed. I ranted. I pouted. I was about to fire off a nastygram reply, but I didn't. I calmed down. I sat on the porch and looked out over the lake and watched a pair of ospreys circle and dive, circle and dive, floating on the updrafts, plunging headlong into the lake to seize dinner.

After a while I reread the note, "The constitutional convention was not a model of strategic planning, but rather a messy affair." *Messy!* That was it! Messy. The very best strategic planning sessions I ever participated in or facilitated were messy affairs. Lots of to-ing and fro-ing. Lots of going back over old territory. Lots of trial balloons and crazy notions. Yet with a steady hand guiding the messy proceedings, we came up with a plan. We discarded some ideas and saved others for later. We prioritized our best ideas. Finally, we agreed on something, which might not be beautiful, but would work.

I fired off a big "thank you" to Dick and promised him an autographed copy of the book now taking shape in my mind. That word, *messy*, started the book moving. It crystallized my left-brain analysis and right-brain creativity. Dick suggested Madison's complete notes and the *Federalist Papers* as starting points. I was off on my new journey.

Over the months and years that followed, I read, researched, haunted historic homes, sites, and archives, and surfed the Internet. I extracted the strategic planning techniques the framers used and tried to get inside their minds as they struggled to create their plan. I became especially fond of James Madison; visited his home twice, lingered in his little Roman temple, and contemplated his grave. It was there that I noticed the date he died, June 28, 1836. Wow! My birthday is June 28. "What an interesting coincidence," said my left brain. My right brain whistled the theme from the *Twilight Zone* and insisted, "There are no coincidences."

As the project evolved, I decided to move beyond including case studies from my own consulting business to illustrate modern strategic planning approaches that mirror the framers' techniques. I asked three executives to give me their insights on strategic leadership and planning, and they agreed. You'll meet Evan Rees, Greg Swienton, and John Zumwalt, as well as many others. Their stories of strategic leadership are interwoven with the stories of the framers' work before, during, and after the Constitutional Convention.

For me, this has been an incredible journey. My near-obsession with James Madison, his cohorts, and their exploits helped me escape the prison of my depression. Unleashing my creativity did bring me back to life, gave me new purpose and drive, and opened up new possibilities as I look at everything through the historical lens I discovered. Interviewing and continuing to talk to contemporary executives was an unparalleled leadership mentoring program. My own business flourished as I applied what I learned from these leaders, "ancient or modern."[2]

Some of the leaders I interviewed moved on to new endeavors. Some faced public criticism. Like the framers, these executives are human. We can learn from imperfect leaders precisely because they are like everyone else at this basic level.

A few months after Dick Perles penned his catalytic note on the messiness of the Constitutional Convention, his wife called. Dick had died peacefully in his sleep. Farewell, friend. And thank you, Jemmy Madison, you brought me back to life.[3]

Rebecca Staton-Reinstein

Preamble

"It is only in our united character, as an empire, that our independence is acknowledged, that our power can be regarded, or our credit supported among foreign nations...[Dissolve the union, and] we shall be left nearly in a state of nature, or we may find by our unhappy experience that there is a natural and necessary progression from the extreme of anarchy to the extreme of tyranny, that arbitrary power is most easily established on the ruins of liberty abused to licentiousness."

– George Washington[1]

Successful leaders know they need a strong, strategic plan to get through times both tough and good. They know the only way to save a company, or a country, is to implement that plan relentlessly and modify it when necessary. Strategic leaders *respond* to crises, while others *react* with tactics. Strategic leaders decide when it's time to make small course adjustments or go in a new direction based on thoughtful analysis.

Tough times are nothing new for leaders. Leaders are defined by the hard challenges they take on and how they tackle them. The leaders you'll meet in this book, whether from the twenty-first or the eighteenth centuries, share two characteristics: they have *vision* and they *execute strategic plans to make that vision a reality.*

A Tale of Two Meetings

The executives gathered around the table were glum. The local economy was tanking. Companies all over town were shedding staff like dandruff. The normal boardroom banter was absent. The only sound was the clink of silver spoons on china cups. For the first time, they felt the full weight of the fate of the company settle on their fashionably-clad shoulders.

Then the CEO arrives, dapper and chipper, a smile on his face. He accepts his herbal tea from the concierge, raises his cup in salute, and starts the meeting.

"Folks, we're going to be OK. Our plan is working and will get us through this." The bold statement is greeted by facial expressions from shock to relief, from wonder to knowing confidence. The CEO explains how the robust strategic plan they forged months ago will carry them through this rough patch. They will dial back a few targets, go full steam ahead on others, add some staff, and continue to follow their plan. He ends by saying, "Our competitors are floundering and grasping at gimmicks. Our plan has saved the company."

* * * * * * * *

Go back in time to 1787. Sunlight seeps through the shuttered windows of an elegantly appointed room with hand-carved furniture. The stylishly dressed men in their silks, fine woolens, and linens hardly notice their surroundings. Outside the stuffy, hot room, the economy is tanking, inflation is rampant, violence due to foreclosures is common, and enemies encroach, waiting to attack. The fate of their country is at stake.

Then the host of the gathering rises and begins to speak to the glum delegates. "Gentlemen, our country is in peril, but we have a plan to save her and put us firmly on the road to a sound future that we have paid such a heavy price to secure." He reads a plan for organizing a national government based on the principles embraced by the majority of people in the room. Their faces register shock as they realize they will not be amending the existing framework, but planning an entirely new form of government. Some fidget and scowl, some smile in exultation, others simply look bewildered. Most shoot a glance at the most prominent man in the room, General George Washington. He nods his approval as each idea is read. Hope spreads through the room as the delegates realize that the bold new plan can save their country.

* * * * * * * * *

When the Going Gets Tough...

The founding fathers[2] and the contemporary leaders in this book, despite their similarities, have one crucial difference — the modern leaders are not trying to create a nation. Yet the modern leaders were chosen because, when they had to make tough decisions, they acted strategically, as did the founders. They saw a future many others could not see. They set a new course and mobilized their teams. Since the original interviews were conducted, some of the leaders have moved on, and some have stumbled.

What they said and accomplished is frozen in time, just as with the founding fathers. The contemporary leaders readily admitted they made mistakes and shared how they learned from them. We can learn from them *because* they are so human.

When author and historian Joseph Ellis describes the founding fathers, he also might be describing modern leaders:

> This is a story, then, about tragedy as well as triumph, indeed about their mutual and inextricable coexistence. I come away from it still believing that the gathering of political talent at this historical moment is unlikely ever to be surpassed...But I also come away with a more chastened sense of celebration, periodically wishing that the founders had been demigods who could perform miracles. Then I catch myself and realize that, *if flawless, they would have nothing to teach us. And they do.*[3]

The way the framers of the U.S. Constitution went about creating their plan of government has many parallels with the way modern leaders engage in strategic planning. In many ways, the Constitutional Convention was a strategic planning session.

In this book, you will experience that tumultuous time over two hundred years ago and gain an understanding of the awful circumstances that compelled leaders to confront the status quo and, technically, commit treason for the second time. Along the way, you'll meet leaders of today and see how they confront challenges and develop strategies parallel to the methodology of the framers and founders.

Meet the Contemporary Leaders

Meet these men and women who led their organizations through tough times:[4]

- **B. Ben Baldanza**, CEO, **Spirit Airlines**: Since 2005, he has helped the airline grow in a turbulent industry, replacing the aging fleet, competing as a low-cost carrier, and building an international presence at its home airport.

- **David L. Brown**, former City Manager, **Coral Gables, Florida**: From 2001-2008, he led the city into the digital age by providing greater services and improved operational efficiency to its forty-four thousand residents.[5]

- **George Hanbury II**, COO/Executive Vice President, **Nova Southeastern University**: He's recreating Thomas Jefferson's 'academical village' on the NSU campus. He came to the university in 1998 after serving as a city manager and turning around several declining cities.

- **Steven D. Hayworth**, Chairman/CEO, **Gibraltar Private Bank and Trust**: He founded the bank in 1994 and grew it from $40 million to $1 billion in eleven years. The bank thrived in a highly competitive niche while others failed. **Tony Caron** served as CFO.[6]

- **Steven D. Hickman**, President/CEO, **Florida Shores Bank – Southeast**: Hickman started this commercial bank in 2006 with a business model for long-term growth that is focused on the needs of underserved small businesses in the Pompano Beach, Florida area.

- **Michael Howe**, former CEO, **MinuteClinic**.[7] From 2005 to 2008, he worked to change the face of health care, writing a new prescription for an ailing industry, and growing the business from nineteen retail clinics to five hundred twenty-five.

- **Luda Kopeikina**, Founder, CEO, **Noventra Corporation**: She founded the company in 1999 to promote companies with innovative technologies. She also developed a breakthrough executive decision-making methodology.

- **Alan Levine**, former CEO, **Broward Health**: In 2006, he took over a hospital system facing the healthcare crisis and local calamities and restored its vitality. He is now Louisiana's secretary of Health and Hospitals.

- **Edward Novak**, former Senior Vice President, **Bank of America**: He built a strong team to improve operational support for the commercial division, while managing technology in an ever-changing financial marketplace.

- **Clarence Otis**, CEO, **Darden Restaurants**: In 2004, he set out to create a new type of customer experience and redefine the casual dining niche in signature restaurants such as Red Lobster.

- **Howard Putnam**, former CEO, **Southwest Airlines**: In 1978, founder Herb Kelleher faced brutal competition and brought Putnam aboard to take charge of the flying experience. Putnam did, *and* tripled profitability.

- **Evan Rees**, former President, **CNL Bank**: He left his long career as a bank executive in 2008 and took on the challenge of entrepreneurship to raise money for a variety of nonprofits.

- **Donna Shalala**, President, **University of Miami**: The former secretary of Health and Human Services in the Clinton administration took the helm at UM in 2001, with a mission to build an economic engine for the community.

- **Stephanie Sonnabend**, co-CEO, President, **Sonesta International Hotels Corporation**: In 2003, she took on the mission of refreshing the brand and growing the business by creating unique hotels that reflect local culture.

- **John Stunson**, City Manager, **Oakland Park, Florida**: He began a second stint as city manager in 2001, facing major survival problems for the city of forty-three thousand. He created new community leadership structures.

- **Gregory Swienton**, Chairman/CEO, **Ryder System**: As CEO since 2000, he has led the company in a fresh approach to sustained profitability in a highly competitive market, while building a strong culture.

- **Stephen Tansey**, COO, **York Container Company**: Since becoming COO in 2004, he helped the family

-owned manufacturer adopt new management structures and adapt to a changing regional economy.

- **Timothy Winger**, Owner/CEO, **Novelty Manufacturing**: He needed to reinvent the family business that was struggling to compete in a market dominated by big-box stores and offshore manufacturing.
- **John Zumwalt III**, Chairman/CEO, **PBSJ Corporation**: When he became CEO of the subsidiary, PBS&J International, he set an ambitious goal "to be the first billion-dollar company with a culture."

As these leaders encountered tough situations, they took a strategic approach, very much like the Constitutional framers. Both groups followed similar steps to translate vision into reality at critical junctures. They:

- Acknowledged the magnitude of the issues without flinching;
- Focused their own strengths and those of their teams to face the issues head-on;
- Envisioned a different and better future for their organizations;
- Put strategic plans in place, and focused on results relentlessly;
- Avoided the pitfalls of knee-jerk, firefighting reactions to obstacles that would have diverted them from their goals;
- Kept everyone focused and energized; and,
- Made tough, necessary decisions and acted on them.

As a result, these contemporary leaders, like the founding

fathers, created organizations that could survive and eventually thrive in a hostile world. To understand that world of some two hundred years ago... [8]

* * * * * * * * *

The Crisis

Imagine a cool, early spring evening in 1787. Edmund Randolph, Governor of Virginia, and James Madison are ensconced in high-backed chairs before the fire. The Governor's well-tailored silk suit shimmers in the reflected firelight of his elegantly appointed study. He lounges in his chair, sipping mulled wine. Madison, dressed in his customary black garb, his face intense, sits forward, his small frame alive with energy that crackles behind his solemn countenance. The Revolution may have been over for four years, but their conversation swirls around the dire state of their fledgling nation.

Madison addresses his host, "Edmund, I tell you this new convention must work! Just this morning, the papers reported those damned pirates have captured another of our ships in the Mediterranean. Jefferson tells me we're losing a quarter of our grain and fish exports to them. Did you know they're holding the captain for ransom and selling the crew into slavery? The government simply cannot do anything about it. General Washington is fed up and thinks it could all collapse. He's told me we need to act."

"I know, Jemmy," Randolph responds somewhat hesitantly, "but I'm not convinced this meeting you've proposed in Philadelphia will be any more productive than the one we went to in Annapolis last year. It did cool down our Virginia hotheads who wanted to declare war on Maryland and Delaware over our fishing rights. But I'm more afraid of being picked off by the Europeans."

He segues into the British refusal to abandon their frontier garrisons as required in the treaty that ended the Revolution.

He says he mistrusts the French despite their help in defeating the British. He worries about Spain's complex maneuverings in the west. "I'm getting frustrated talking about it," he continues. "Why do you think this meeting will help? He stands, takes a few paces, and returns to his chair with a sigh.

"Because, Edmund, we don't have a choice," Madison says, trying to control his own rising anxiety. "The system we have now *does not work*." He comes to the subject that has alarmed people throughout the states, Shays' Rebellion. "If these farm foreclosures continue, Captain Shays and his rebels will become the norm. The very fact that they took over the courts, ran off the judges, and attacked the arsenal threatens all of us."

"But look what my cousin Jefferson wrote to William Smith," Randolph says as he takes a letter from his pocket, holds it closer to the firelight and reads. " 'Where does this anarchy consist? And can history produce an instance of rebellion so honorable conducted? God forbid that we should ever be twenty years without such a rebellion. What signify a few lives lost? The tree of liberty must be refreshed from time to time with the blood of patriots and tyrants.' " He waves the letter disgustedly and returns it to his pocket.[9]

"Yes, everyone's quoting that letter," Madison sighs. "Tom's been in Paris too long. He doesn't understand the threat here. When I spoke with General Washington, he was furious about the rebellion and the reaction of those New Englanders. They called for a virtual monarchy to keep it from happening again. All of this should spur some of the fence-sitters to come to Philadelphia and act.

"Anyway, we're all threatened by this rampant inflation because the states keep issuing worthless paper money. Who knows what violence will come next?" The firelight illuminates the fear creeping into his face.

"Of course we're right to be scared, Jemmy. I heard a rumor that some states are planning to secede," Randolph says, his voice beginning to rise.

"Edmund, the picture's grim. With our unpaid war debts, the Europeans won't lend us more money. But I have a plan to make this Convention succeed. As I see it, we must abandon the current Articles of Confederation..."

Randolph sits up abruptly and sputters, "But Jemmy, that's treason..."

Madison interrupts, "It's not the first time we are guilty of *that* crime. We didn't hang in the Revolution and we won't hang now." Randolph's eyes widen with alarm as he puts down his glass and leans forward nervously. "Hear me out, Edmund. For the last year, I've read everything on governance I can lay my hands on — even my old college papers. The type of confederation we have has always collapsed and failed. The States cannot be the center of sovereignty..."

Randolph breaks in again, his voice cracking, "But Jemmy, you're talking about *my* job now. As Governor, I have to defend the rights of the states..."

"Hear me out, Edmund. My studies of every form of government — from ancient to modern — tell me that only a strong republican form can survive..."[10]

Agitated, Randolph interrupts again, "But our country is too big. I may not be the scholar you are, Jemmy, but everybody knows republics collapse when the territory becomes too big. They turn to despotism and worse. Look at the Roman Empire..."

Madison leaps to his feet, his face alive, and takes his debating stance. "That's been true in the past, but I believe we can construct a republic that can be contained though checks and balances with three separate branches of government. All the great political philosophers of the last two centuries agree on those principles. Look at the British constitution. It enshrines..."

Randolph suppresses a laugh, "Now you're *really* being treasonous!"

Madison ignores the joke and keeps talking, "We must put together a national system, not beholden to the states, but to the people themselves, with a strong executive branch. Just read over my draft, Edmund, because I want you to present it when the convention opens."

"Me? But..."

Madison speaks more intently. "You're the host of the Convention. They'll expect you to start the session with some sort of outline. You'll present the plan from our Virginia delegation as the suggested form of government. We are the largest and most powerful state, so we should use it to our advantage."

"But Jemmy, if word of this gets out..." Randolph's voice trails off as he glances at the study doors.

"Don't worry; I'm working on The General." Madison's tone becomes conspiratorial as he sits down and leans toward the governor. "If General Washington is there, we're all covered. No one will doubt *his* patriotism and intent. You'll appoint The General to the state delegation immediately. As more state leaders agree to come, he'll see the necessity of showing up.

"Besides, 'states rights' men like Patrick Henry will boycott it. They're perfectly happy with the status quo. Let Henry and his cronies stay in Richmond until they rot! Do you know he refuses to be part of the delegation? He says he 'smelled a rat.'"

"Jemmy, I've never seen you so worked up."

Madison is on his feet again, pacing before the fire. "Worked up? You bet I'm worked up. It's too bad John Adams is in London and Tom's in Paris. But Alexander Hamilton will be there, and he's such a radical our proposals will look sensible, not treasonous!

"Listen, the chaos and breakdown are escalating. The Articles of Confederation and Congress are impotent. Everything we fought for in the Revolution will be destroyed. Who knows when another country will have the courage to create such an experiment in liberty?"

"OK, Jemmy, I'll read your draft. Maybe it will be cooler in Philadelphia this summer anyway..."

* * * * * * * * *

The Future at Stake

When fifty-five men eventually assembled in Philadelphia from May through September in 1787, they knew the future of their country was at stake. They represented twelve of the thirteen states — Rhode Island refused to send delegates. Travel back to the Pennsylvania State House, now Independence Hall, in that long-ago spring and summer. Enter the meeting room with its classic Georgian architecture and muted colors, where the green baize-covered tables are arranged in a semicircle facing a raised platform. The tables, seating two men each, are arranged geographically from north to south as in the Congress, beginning with Massachusetts and ending with Georgia.

General George Washington sits at the table on the platform. His unanimous election as president of the Constitutional Convention and his grave air lend legitimacy to the proceedings. Washington plays a key role in these proceedings, although, as it turns out, he does not speak publicly to any issue during the entire summer until the last day. Even when sitting with his Virginia delegation, when the Convention meets as a Committee of the Whole, he retains his enigmatic silence.

Every eye in the room watches for his reactions as they speculate endlessly about his views. Does a raised eyebrow mean he's suppressing his legendary temper? Does the flicker of an eyelid signify mild disagreement? Does a slight relaxing of his closed mouth indicate he approves? Behind the scenes he is more forthcoming.

Men like James Madison have come to know and appreciate his strong republican views. The General's beliefs carry weight and inspire the younger leaders in the fight for a strong national government.

Great Leaders Mold Their Teams

The men we reverentially call the "framers" and Thomas Jefferson called "demigods" were an interesting, if skewed, collection of American leaders. Staunch opponents of change, like Patrick Henry of Virginia, either stayed home, or actively sought to derail the proceedings from a distance like New York's Governor Clinton, who had two of his henchmen in the state's three-man delegation.

New York sent Alexander Hamilton, John Lansing, and Robert Yates. When the latter two Clinton allies realized the new Constitution would decrease the power of the states, they left, never to return. The delegation rules prevented Alexander Hamilton from casting his single vote for the state and he also left, but later returned.[11]

The delegates were a diverse group of lawyers, major land owners, scholars, diplomats, and legislators, with a sprinkling of men of humble origin, most notably Benjamin Franklin and Alexander Hamilton. Most were men of property and social standing. A number were slave owners; others were active in antislavery causes. Many had seen service in the Revolution. They were the seasoned, recognized leaders of their day. They ran the gamut from brilliant to dull, from morally upstanding to corrupt, from well-intentioned to purposely destructive, from passionate to indifferent. They were used to representing the people, but were not representative *of* the people.

Modern leaders may inherit a team that is not ideal and it may not be feasible to replace all the members. Like Madison, Washington, and the other Convention leaders, strong leaders of today can mold a less-than-ideal group into a more effective team by keeping everyone focused on the vision and mission, as later chapters will show.

In the end, the men at the Convention, like the best of today's executive teams, managed to transcend their immediate personal, parochial interests. They created the U.S. Constitution and a strong system of government that have stood for over two hundred years, in spite of the frailties of the humans who created them and who must make them work. Contemporary teams often demonstrate this same sort of synergy and unexpectedly strong results.

Put Yourself in the Picture

See yourself as part of your state delegation debating, dining, and discovering Philadelphia with Alexander Hamilton, Benjamin Franklin, James Madison, or George Washington, as you work through those crucial months in 1787. The enormous windows in the high-ceilinged meeting room are closed and shuttered against the prying eyes and ears of the public and the press.

You meet from ten a.m. until three p.m. without a break. You sit on an uncushioned wooden chair, straining to hear. The city put down sand to dampen the clang of hooves and the creaking of wagon wheels on the busy cobblestone street outside, but the measure is only partially effective.

In the front of the room, James Madison hunches over a table, scratching away in shorthand with a quill pen, trying to record everything that is said. He wants the world to have a record of *how* a republican constitution is created. He seldom takes a break and is never absent. Some delegates disappear for weeks at a time. You all have pressing business and family matters back home.

You're spending your own money. Your state legislature had no idea you'd need to be supported for so long. Because there is no standard currency, you need to have Spanish, Dutch, or English coins — local merchants won't accept your state's worthless paper money.

Yet just like a contemporary business meeting, socializing is important. At four o'clock, delegates assemble in one of the taverns for the main meal of the day. You dine on fresh meats, fish, fruit, vegetables, pastries, and delicacies washed down with ale, beer, cider, *and* wine. Afterwards you smoke your pipe or cigar, drink port, and swap bawdy stories and political views.

Some evenings you're off to the theater, a concert, or an edifying lecture. You tour botanical gardens, factories, and museums. You attend church services to hear famous preachers from various denominations. You write long letters to friends, family, and political allies.

As you sit, month after month, in the sweltering Pennsylvania State House, you are frustrated as some point you already decided is brought up yet again. You chafe under the self-imposed decision of complete secrecy. You are worn out from working six days a week in the Convention, doing committee work, sharing a sleeping room with a fellow delegate who snores prodigiously, eating and drinking too much and exercising too little, and generally disrupting your life.

Yet despite fatigue, flies, and frayed tempers, you slowly transform the interests and pet ideas of a diverse group into a coherent plan for republican governance. You sacrifice, compromise, and stand your ground as you face a set of challenges that could destroy your new nation. You overcome all obstacles and create something unique.

Leadership makes the difference.

Great Leaders' Motto: Be Prepared

In today's volatile business environment, companies act or react in varying ways. Some thrash about, looking for a quick fix or new marketing campaign. Some hunker down, cut staff and costs, and put all their energies into short-term survival. Some do whatever Wall Street analysts suggest, eking out a few more pennies on the stock price and keeping their jobs for another quarter. A few resort to fraud.

Some companies *do* stay strategically focused and succeed over the long haul. They look to the future and move steadily in that direction. They invest, plan, and prepare for expansion.

Preparation separates successful planners from unsuccessful ones. Although it's hard to imagine, there are executives who show up without doing their homework. Like Madison and a handful of others who arrived in Philadelphia with a written plan, successful leaders have a purpose, a direction, and a draft plan. Even the majority of the fifty-five delegates who didn't come with a draft plan had all done some serious situational analysis, which was why they were attending.

James Madison deserves his title as "Father of the Constitution" not because of his influence on its content, but because of his methodical planning. He made himself a constitutional expert with detailed research and analysis. He outlined a governing constitution that became the de facto agenda for the Convention. His draft organized the debates into some semblance of order around the key questions that required decisions, although the finished plan differed from his in significant ways.

Madison's behind-the-scenes work led to compromises that helped the Convention succeed. The framers, like modern executives, entered the session with some fixed ideas and some areas where they were flexible. In a good strategic planning session like the Convention, ideas flow and morph, are rehashed and reshaped, and end up stronger and different, if not perfect, in the final plan. This messiness is necessary to bring out better, more creative, ideas. Successful modern leaders do the same as Madison. They spend time before the planning session putting together ideas, discuss those ideas with the team, and get people on board.

Great Leaders Lead by Example

Despite his misgivings, Governor Randolph presented the draft at the opening of the Convention as the "Virginia Plan," and set the stage for the historic planning session. Madison also used his considerable persuasive powers on George

Washington, as did others, convincing him to attend as head of the Virginia delegation.

Washington's presence was crucial to provide protective cover and an atmosphere of legitimacy for the delegates. They were about to violate the Articles of Confederation, which required all thirteen states to agree to any amendments, a feat that had proven impossible. To the shock of many delegates, as soon as the Virginia Plan was presented, it was obvious that they were going to create an entirely new Constitution rather than try to tinker with the existing one.

When John Rutledge seconded Washington's nomination to be president of the Convention, the South Carolina delegate observed, "the presence of General Washington forbids any [negative] observations on the occasion."[12] The General was almost universally revered at this time. Without his presence, many states would not have attended and the Convention would have had little hope of succeeding. In addition, his views were the same as those of Madison at the time and the others who supported a strong national government to replace the supreme power of the states.

Like Washington, contemporary leaders send strong messages to their teams by their presence and conduct at the planning session. If they are engaged and enthusiastic, the team follows suit. If they are going through the motions or undermining the event in some way, the team follows *that* lead.

As Madison records, Washington set the tone for the convention and his style of leadership when he was "conducted to the chair...from which in a very emphatic manner he thanked the Convention for the honor conferred on him, reminded them of the novelty of the scene of business in which he was to act and lamented his want of better qualifications, and claimed the indulgence of the House towards the involuntary errors which his inexperience might occasion."[13]

Extraordinary Times Require Extraordinary Leadership

The framers were involved in a strategic planning session that had both the form and substance of the sessions many leaders conduct today. (The major difference was the *length* of the session.) You can learn from these extraordinary leaders how to create your own enduring organizations, and solve seemingly intractable problems, especially in tough economic times.

As you try to put yourself into that long-ago setting, look at *how* they developed their strategic plan, the Constitution, and use these lessons as guidelines for your own organizations. Look at *how* contemporary leaders, even in situations very different from yours, develop their plans and take their organizations forward.

Perhaps the most important lessons for contemporary leaders come from the extensive, *messy* dialogues about the complex issues of the day. The Convention discussions provide an object lesson in how to encourage creativity through the constructive clash of ideas. They show us how to apply long-term thinking, knowledge of human psychology, and the immediate need for action in pragmatic, useful ways. They also show us how even great leaders can make big mistakes. At the same time, we can also learn from modern leaders, who are as adept as the framers in using the same approaches in discussions, decision-making, and decisive planning.

Listen to these leaders' voices, past and present, as they translate vision into action and successful results. But questions arise: How do you apply these leaders' "*conventional*" wisdom? How do you lead your organization into an extraordinary future? How do you act as a strategic leader when you face a daunting reality? Why is facing reality such an important first step?

Article I

Deal With the Real

Edmund Randolph "then commented on the difficulty of the crisis and the necessity of preventing the fulfillment of the prophecies of the American downfall."[1]

As Edmund Randolph, the 34-year-old governor of Virginia and host of the Constitutional Convention, gaveled the meeting to order on an otherwise idyllic May morning in 1787, the so-called United States were barely united and faced multiple crises of gargantuan proportions. Britain, France, and Spain were keeping up the pressure, hoping to tip the young, weak nation over the edge so they could swoop in and divide up the spoils. Inflation was spiraling out of control as states printed their own worthless paper money. Boundary disputes were escalating among some states, while others were considering withdrawing from the disintegrating confederacy and allying themselves with one of the European powers. Violence was boiling over more frequently. Governor Randolph's opening remarks to the Constitutional Convention, "on the difficulty of the crisis and the necessity of preventing the fulfillment of the prophecies of the American downfall,"[2] were understatements.

There was great interest in what was about to transpire within the Pennsylvania Statehouse as the fifty-five delegates trickled in from all but one state.[3] But the media of the day were frustrated by the gag rules the delegates imposed upon themselves. This didn't stop the newspapers from printing totally fabricated stories or wild rumors from circulating. In fact, had today's tabloid journalists and bloggers managed to sneak inside, these incendiary headlines might have appeared:

- 55 Commit Treason for Second Time
- Top Secret Session Bars Press
- Political Elite Plots Government Overthrow
- Revolutionary Patriot Warns, "I Smell A Rat!"
- Top General Plans Military Coup

Luckily for the delegates (and us), no scandalmongers penetrated the veil of secrecy; most delegates remained discreet, even long after the event.

What can leaders today learn from these men? In what ways are the framers similar to contemporary executives? How are modern leaders, even unknowingly, still using the methods that made the framers so successful in crafting a constitution? In what ways are the approaches of the American founders and framers relevant in today's global economy and in organizations struggling with a very different reality?

A Common Denominator

Reality. That's the common denominator. Leaders, then and now, understand that they must deal with reality, with the world as they find it, not as they wish it. It was that unflinching stance that enabled the framers to spend four months hammering out the necessary compromises to prevent the prophecies of the American downfall from becoming a reality. And it is the same unflinching willingness to face the facts that distinguishes successful strategic leaders today.

The leaders who stepped forward in 1787 had much in common with today's executives. As you picture that room of long ago, imagine something a little different. Instead of their eighteenth-century fashions with lace-trimmed shirts, knee breeches, white stockings, buckled shoes, and long hair or wigs, imagine them in golf shirts, slacks, comfortable shoes, and modern haircuts. Take them off their historic pedestals and out of stiff poses we remember in those dramatic paintings. Picture them sitting comfortably, chatting with you. Put them in your own conference room discussing ideas, arguing passionately, floating trial balloons, playing devil's advocate, becoming excited or growing bored.

When you begin to see them as regular people, it's easier to relate to and learn from them. Most of them were busy executives who ran their own businesses, whether law firms, plantations, or real estate companies. In addition, they had held public office or served as judges, often at their own expense. They managed budgets, property, staff, vendors, and contracts.

They had busy social lives and maintained voluminous correspondence. Their daily consumption of alcohol would leave most of us woozy, but they looked down on drunkenness and were seldom even tipsy. Their diet would leave us sluggish, yet most of them were physically active, walking or riding on horseback miles every day. George Washington was noted for his superb horsemanship, physical strength, and endurance, but even frail James Madison rode well and could stay in the saddle for long hours of rough riding when necessary. Only a handful of the men would be considered obese.

They devoured newspapers, periodicals, and books, and stayed abreast of local, national, and international affairs. They were curious and followed scientific, medical, and agricultural developments closely. Many spoke or wrote several languages, and all knew history well. Most supported families that often included several generations and various relatives. They were up early, worked hard, and accomplished much.

Like busy executives today, they faced enormous challenges and knew they must come up with innovative solutions. They understood change was inevitable and knew they must lead it or be overwhelmed by it. They also were realists when it came to human nature. In those days before Sigmund Freud, pop psychology, and so-called reality shows, they had no illusions about how deplorably people could behave. They were living through an extraordinarily tumultuous period and saw exactly how well and poorly people can act when put to the test.

One of their most important traits was a willingness to

face facts. As Governor Randolph opened the Constitutional Convention, he cataloged the dire deterioration of the Confederation, and how it spurred the calling of the convention. Today's successful executives and their teams use the same system — beginning their strategic planning with a thorough analysis of the current situation.

The Real Reality Show

Modern teams seek to understand the realities of their unique context. Their analyses can vary from a single page to a volume thick with supporting documentation. The analyses usually contain data about critical financial indicators, markets, the economy, customers, stakeholders and shareholders, product and service performance, accomplishments and failures, quality and productivity, trends, and other facts to help the team grapple with reality.

Many of the executives you'll meet in this book head organizations that faced major problems and even crises, putting their futures at stake. Several of the executives took over organizations that were declining or had a poor public image. Others were in dramatically shifting markets that demanded the company reinvent itself to survive. Several of these leaders were involved in startups that needed to get established quickly in a very competitive market. Three were city managers who had to turn around the fortunes of struggling urban areas. Like the framers, they were willing to confront the prophecies of downfall.

Gibraltar Private Bank and Trust provides an example of the power of facing reality and acting on this situational analysis to succeed. Gibraltar, a private bank initially serving South Florida, was founded and led by a charismatic and energetic executive, Steve Hayworth, as CEO. The bank, then known as Gibraltar Bank, had catapulted to the top of its niche market in just a few years. As it expanded dramatically, the entrepreneurial executive team members began to feel severe growing pains. From the founding handful of people, the bank now had over one hundred employees and would soon swell to two hundred.

Hayworth and Tony Caron, then CFO, knew the bank could not continue on its present course. Like the framers, they examined the facts. Competitors were beginning to recover from Gibraltar Bank's onslaught. Running an established corporation was different from growing a startup. "People problems" were cropping up. Turnover was starting to take its toll. A trusted manager decamped under a cloud. Executives focused on their own departments and teamwork was weak. The board was willing to support internal development as it searched for the right strategic partner, one which shared their philosophy and provided complementary services. The executives needed to assure their wealthy clientele the bank would maintain the high level of personal service and attention clients had come to expect.

SWOT the Situation

The first task facing the Gibraltar executive team was to analyze its situation with a great deal of depth, precision, and honesty. Caron gathered financial and growth data and asked the other executives to complete departmental analyses. The team produced a rigorous situational analysis that laid out the reality in clear, straightforward terms. In their initial planning session, they performed a no-holds-barred SWOT analysis of their internal **S**trengths and **W**eaknesses, as well as the external **O**pportunities and **T**hreats. Instead of looking at some disturbing data and making excuses or pointing fingers, most of the team immediately tapped their entrepreneurial strengths and started figuring out what they should do.

Hayworth and Caron explain it this way:

Steve Hayworth: First and foremost, we had to understand where we were as an organization and confront the 'brutal facts'[4] and then articulate, without mass chaos, where we wanted to go. Going through the situational analysis helped us get back inside the corral. We had a lot of great ideas, and we had to choose the most important ones.

Tony Caron: After six years, we're still following the same format of our original retreat. We do a situational analysis and all the players review it prior to the session. Then, during the offsite, we do a SWOT analysis. We also identify MIFs [most important factors] and rank them. It really ends up being a consensus and keeps everybody on the same page to do the right thing for the organization. When you do that with the strategic planning process, everybody knows what's happening and gets on board. You just start doing it. I think, particularly when you have a lot of turmoil in an industry, that's even more reason to spend more time more frequently on strategic planning and the process.

In 2005, Gibraltar Bank became an affiliate partner of a respected wealth management public holding company. Gibraltar Bank changed its name to Gibraltar Private Bank and Trust. When it decided to expand into the New York market, the bank did rely on the holding company's extensive analysis and performed its own SWOT. Caron reports:

It just makes sense that performing a SWOT before entering new markets will help lay a solid foundation for growth, as opposed to doing it after the fact. It will save a lot of grief. It has helped us look at things we had not considered before. It gives us a disciplined approach to growth and profit. Just as important, it allows us a disciplined approach to discuss issues we might not have control over and think about what we can do to help negate the downside.

At about the same time Gibraltar Private was moving into the New York market, another experienced banker, Steven Hickman, founded Florida Shores Bank. He planned to focus on the extensive and strong South Florida small business community. Although in a different developmental stage and serving a different target market than Gibraltar Private, Hickman, the CEO, used the same methodology:

> I took what I've learned from being in charge of strategic planning in other banks and put all of that work into this plan. I like to do a SWOT analysis and put our Strengths, Weaknesses, Opportunities, and Threats in that context and build from it. That has worked for me and gets a lot of input from everyone. I'm the conductor, but I'll let them build it. I've added some things too; a competitive scan, an economic scan, and a market scan. I bring all those resources to the table, but the real driver is the SWOT.

Facing hard facts is not always obvious to a company. York Container Company, founded in 1954, is now owned by two of the three founding families. For most of its history, York was quite successful. It supplied corrugated containers, point-of-sale displays, and design services to manufacturers located within a few hundred miles of York, Pennsylvania. The corrugated packaging industry is considered mature, although many companies try to distinguish themselves through the use of high-end graphics. As some regional manufacturers began to shift their production offshore, York began to feel the impact of globalization.

As York Container was making a generational shift in its day-to-day management, the company brought in a family-business consultant who helped it look at the facts in a new way. His analysis showed the company's growth had actually been flat for several years and sales were declining. At about that time, the son-in-law of one of the owners came into the company. Steve Tansey had an MBA from the Wharton School of the University of Pennsylvania, and some solid business experience. Although he modestly claims to have been lucky and to have built on others' accomplishments, he served as a strong catalyst to help York face its harsh reality and make many of the necessary changes to continue its decades of success.

Tansey began with a SWOT analysis and helped the executive leadership team focus on a different set of metrics and analyses that could help them make better decisions. As he gained recognition for his expertise, he helped reorganize York Container's financial and production functions. He built on the existing staff's depth of knowledge and brought in new managers with fresh ideas from outside companies and industries. When he became chief operating officer, he revitalized the executive team's planning process and helped the managing owners focus on greater analysis of results. It was a daunting task. But Tansey's steady focus and consistent message, to "look at the facts and understand their meaning," took hold. Slowly, as the results of his methodical approach became obvious, his influence grew, and York Container's growth rebounded.

Ignore the Facts at Your Peril

Other companies are not as fortunate as York Container; many consistently ignore the facts and almost destroy themselves in the process. They behave more like the state legislators and officials in the 1780s who disregarded facts and opposed any changes to the governing Articles of Confederation or the supremacy of individual state power. The powerful governor of New York, George Clinton, and the most powerful politician in Virginia, Patrick Henry, tried to scuttle the Constitutional Convention and the ratification process. Most historians agree that the struggling new nation could not survive and had to transform itself.

Savvy leaders in every generation from the early republic to the present use these strategic approaches. They:

- Gather the pertinent data;
- Stand back and examine the facts dispassionately, without denying or whining;
- Interpret the meaning behind the facts correctly; and,
- Resist the urge to ignore things they don't like, cast blame, or weasel out of their responsibilities.

These are the minimum starting points. It's where the framers started and where successful CEOs and their teams start. They deal with the real. They prioritize and analyze company strengths, weaknesses, opportunities, and threats. The most important elements from the analysis become the basis for their plans. They decide *how* they will build on their most powerful internal strengths and make use of external opportunities. In fact, this is a hallmark of successful strategic leaders. They put concrete plans in place to make the most of what they have going for them. Next, they look at *how* they will mitigate the most powerful internal weaknesses and external threats. Analyzing risk is second nature to most leaders.

For example, Gibraltar Bank surveyed its employees in 2002. It found that one of its greatest strengths was a dedicated workforce, while a weakness was the potential for disaffection as the company grew and changed. As the executives built the new strategic plan, they included the creation of a new human resources function that would eventually become a central feature of their planning process. It was charged with building the planning process into job descriptions and performance evaluations. The goal was to help every employee stay engaged in, and contributing to, the bank's goals.

The Framers SWOT Their Situation

Return now to the Convention meeting room where Governor Randolph is running through the current, dire situation. If the delegates had used flip charts and markers, their SWOT analysis might have looked something like Figure 1.

Persuasion is Not Manipulation

The historical record presents another object lesson in preparing for a strategic planning session. James Madison was not only relentless in engineering, with others,[5] the Constitutional Convention, but also in making sure leaders such as Washington would be there to provide thoughtful contributions and legitimacy. He worked with the Virginia delegation to finalize the plan he authored. It would become the framework for the discussion. He was an experienced legislator and effective politician. Having served in the Continental Congress, the Virginia Council of State, and the Virginia Assembly, he was highly effective at working behind the scenes, building coalitions and consensus, influencing others to compromise and take the action, and then letting others put the public face on the matter.

Persuasion is not manipulation. James Madison used persuasion to help people see the value in careful preparation, planning, and execution. Whether debating on the floor of the Constitutional Convention or in the Virginia Ratifying Convention, talking one-on-one with other delegates or writing brilliantly in *The Federalist*,[6] he used arguments that resonated with people. He showed them the facts and the impact of those facts on their lives. He helped them overcome their misgivings and look to the future. He helped them see the positive consequences of a strong central government that still had a place for the interests of the states and the individual.

Effective executives exercise these same skills to build support for planning and change. Consider Novelty

Constitutional Convention SWOT Analysis

Internal Strengths	Internal Weaknesses	External Opportunities	External Threats
Common vision	Many states not paying Congressional assessments; no enforcement and no recourse	France willing to support development	Britain, Spain & France: want U.S. territory
Commitment to republican government	Boundary and commercial disputes among states	Trade in Europe, Mediterranean, Caribbean	U.S. is pawn in European political intrigue
Experience: legislators, governors, judges, lawyers, military service	Shays' Rebellion fed by high inflation and farm foreclosures; Congress has no power to intervene in state disputes or rebellion	Spain wants agreements on Florida, Gulf Coast borders, use of Mississippi	Piracy in Caribbean, Mediterranean
Vast land and natural resources	Pre-war and wartime debt not being repaid	Pent up demand for American raw materials	European creditors not extending credit
Willingness to face reality	No national currency; states issue worthless paper money, driving inflation; foreign hard money in use; no trade policy		England uses debt issue to justify illegal forts on borders
Energetic, people willing to emigrate from other countries	All power held by sovereign states; little support for Confederation Congress; it seldom has a quorum to conduct business		Europeans prevent trade with Europe and Caribbean
Understand human nature	Congress cannot prevent war or support it; cannot punish treaty violations; cannot impose taxes, can only request contributions		
	Some states trying to set up separate deals with foreign powers for commerce; some threaten other countries		

Figure 1

Manufacturing, a maker of garden containers and accessories in Lancaster, Pennsylvania. Tim Winger, CEO and grandson of the founder, never involved his management team in formal planning until his situational analysis showed that, unless he made radical changes, the currently profitable company would not remain viable in the long run. Although he was torn about giving up a family business, he heeded the facts and decided that preparing the company for eventual sale was the best business decision.

Winger told the managers the truth. He laid out the financials and his decision, something almost unheard of in closely-held family businesses. He invited the managers to talk about their reactions honestly, which they did. Then he invited them to help him make the transition happen by creating and executing a plan to grow the company's profitability to make it more attractive for a potential buyer. Because of their trust in him and his ability to persuade rather than dictate, he galvanized them into a team that was ready to take on the challenge.

As the plan they put in place matured, Novelty Manufacturing moved into new markets, changed its business model, and became a different company. Some managers moved on while others stuck with it. Winger succeeded in building a more valuable company and keeping it on track for eventual sale.

To Transform, Face the Facts

Novelty Manufacturing faced a major external threat: for years, the so-called big-box stores dominated its customer base and represented an overwhelming portion of revenue, profit, and commissions. The business strategy of these mega stores is to demand constant price cuts from suppliers to maintain low prices for store customers. Looking at the trends and impact on Novelty's margins, Winger and his team had to face a brutal fact: there would come a point when it would no longer be feasible to meet the price-cutting demands of these biggest customers. Crisis was inevitable without a major change.

It was a tough decision to formulate a new business strategy. Novelty Manufacturing would have to wean itself from the big-box stores and diversify into smaller niche markets, change the product mix, and import some products rather than manufacturing everything. The company would have to reinvent itself. As the head of marketing and sales moaned, only half jokingly, "There go my big commissions!" He was, however, the first to embrace the new strategy enthusiastically and make it work as he sought new markets.

It took several years for Novelty Manufacturing to diversify successfully into a variety of niche markets and reduce its big-box revenue reliance. Winger's gamble to bring his team into the decision-making process has paid off in a more nimble, profitable company — one that is more attractive to potential buyers.

Reality is the Leader's Strategic Partner

Effective leaders build enthusiasm so the planning session is successful. They set the stage for good teamwork, not through artificial exercises, but through good dialog and discussion, give-and-take, persuasion, and joint goals. The team becomes a *team* when they face the facts, and *reality*, together. They look at what they do well and build on it. They look at their challenges and plan, *realistically*, to overcome them.

The delegates who showed up in Philadelphia in 1787 were realists. Whether they thought the Articles of Confederation needed tweaking or were ready to create an entirely new government, they *knew* there must be change. When Hayworth, Caron, Hickman, Tansey, and Winger led their teams through situational analyses, they *knew* their businesses must face a new reality and come up with a different plan than the one that had worked in the past. The eighteenth and twenty-first century leaders did it without flinching.

Now, with their situational analysis completed, leaders and their teams are ready to "create a system without example," in

Madison's words. But to do that, they have to suspend their realism for a while. Can leaders who can stare the crisis straight in the eye without wavering also transform themselves into visionaries? This is the next hurdle for the strategic leader.

Article II

Bring Vision to Reality

"A leader does have to have some vision, and then bring that vision to reality."
— George Hanbury II,
COO and Executive Vice President
Nova Southeastern University

Vision. The very word seems so abstract. Why is it so important in accomplishing great goals? As Yogi Berra supposedly said, "If you don't know where you are going, you will wind up somewhere else." Simply put, without a clear idea of where you want to go, you're at the mercy of fate.

Every business book exhorts leaders to have vision. Every leader interviewed for this book acknowledges the importance of vision. George Hanbury II, the COO and executive vice president of Nova Southeastern University, summed up the theme of this book when he said, "A leader does have to have some vision, and then bring that vision to reality."

The framers of the Constitution shared a vision for the future of the United States. Many of them fought in the American Revolution and in the political arena to make it a reality. Realizing the vision was not becoming reality propelled many of the fifty-five delegates to Philadelphia in the summer of 1787.

Thomas Jefferson's ringing words in the Declaration of Independence captured the founders' republican vision.

> We hold these truths to be self-evident, that all men are created equal, that they are endowed by their Creator with certain unalienable Rights, that among these are

Life, Liberty, and the Pursuit of Happiness – That to secure these rights, Governments are instituted among Men, deriving their just powers from the consent of the governed...

We, therefore, the Representatives of the united States of America...in the Name, and by Authority of the good People of these Colonies, solemnly publish and declare, That these united Colonies are, and of Right ought to be, Free and Independent States...And for the support of this Declaration, with a firm reliance on the protection of Divine Providence, we mutually pledge to each other our Lives, our Fortunes, and our sacred Honor.

The fatally flawed Articles of Confederation could not make this stirring vision a reality. Under the Articles, supreme power resided in the states. The Confederation Congress could not levy taxes; it could only beg the states for money to operate. Congress had no power to enforce any legislation it passed. It could not establish a national currency, pay the Revolutionary war debt owed European creditors, or prevent the states from striking separate deals with foreign powers.

Each state had one vote in the Congress, giving small states and large states the same power. Often one or two small states stymied the will of the majority. Realistically, the Articles could not be amended, because that required agreement by all thirteen states.

Congress had little power, so delegates were often absent and the body went for weeks without a quorum to conduct its business. With economic, political, and social chaos growing and avaricious European powers lurking, it was mandatory to rescue the vision and decide on a new way to make it a reality.

Like the founders, contemporary leaders face the reality of the present *and* develop a clear vision of the future. Howard Putnam took over as the CEO of Southwest Airlines in 1978 at a time when it was beleaguered by creditors and competitors and its vision was being severely challenged.

> When I got there, we had twelve airplanes and a thousand employees. I understood what the challenges were and what my role was. I had to position this little company for the future. One of the first challenges was to figure out quickly what the vision was, what business we were in, and what we were going to be when we grew up.
>
> I took the team of nine senior managers plus Herb Kelleher, the chairman, and myself to a little college conference room that we paid $25 to rent. We even took our own lunches to save money. I said, 'We're not leaving this room until I can write up on the wall behind me, in a hundred words or less, what Southwest Airlines' vision is.' After a Texas barbecue that night, the next morning it came to us in about thirty minutes: 'Hey, we're not an airline. We're in mass transportation!'
>
> We wrote this fifty-two-word statement that was sort of strategic and sort of tactical. A professor told me it was the worst vision statement he'd ever seen. But I told him it didn't make any difference. It was simple and easy to understand...and it worked.

During Putnam's tenure at Southwest, he put that vision statement to work while successfully leading the airline through deregulation. The results were clear: revenues and profits tripled in three years.

John Zumwalt III is CEO and chairman of PBSJ Corporation, one of the largest infrastructure planning, engineering, construction management, architecture, and related services firms in the United States. He served as chairman and CEO of the company's chief subsidiary, PBS&J, from 2005-2007. There he had risen through the ranks, starting as an engineer in 1973 and working his way up to president in 2000. Yet Zumwalt is not a stereotypical engineer, but a visionary of a very different ilk. In accepting an award for promoting diversity, he said, "My vision is to be the first billion-dollar company that still has a culture!" Since taking the reins, he has guided the company along that trajectory.

Zumwalt was influenced by the generation before him, the so-called Greatest Generation — people who survived the Great Depression and World War II and built the new U.S. economy in the 1950s and 1960s. One of the things that struck Zumwalt about that generation, which included the founders of PBS&J, was how involved they were as engineers in their society.

> My vision for the company has two parts. First, we want to grow our services from commodity-based, where price is our only relationship, to higher-value services and prominence in our industry that are relationship-based. The other aspect is to move from just being physically located in a community, having an office and doing some projects, to eventually working with civic leaders and decision makers and being involved outside our profession.
>
> We want to groom community professionals as trusted advisors. We spend time on developing our leadership culture and investing money in community and outreach programs where our offices are located. When you commit to a community, you're doing the first function of a CEO, to be a tie between the company and society.

For Zumwalt, community involvement is not just about doing good, although that outcome certainly benefits the community. Putting his comprehensive vision of community relationships into action also benefits PBS&J.

We have people working on projects on both these fronts. We have a solid presence in the community. We get a sustainable amount of business since we're walking with the right people. We're helping to develop the community programs of tomorrow with our input, and not just sitting there, waiting for the next project to be advertised in the newspaper.

Making a vision a reality has been George Hanbury's trademark. At Nova Southeastern University, he's building one of his most ambitious visions yet, translating Thomas Jefferson's concept of a university as an "academical village" into a reality in Davie, Florida. It's been a long and interesting journey for him.

Hanbury was the first in his family to finish high school and then added another first by attending Virginia Tech (Virginia Polytechnic Institute and State University). Inspired by the launch of the first Sputnik satellite, he started to study engineering, switched to pre law, and finally discovered his vocation, graduating with a degree in public administration. After serving as an assistant city manager in two cities, he began a series of stints as city manager for several Virginia cities. When he arrived, each city faced the challenges of shifting demographics, a declining economy, and urban blight. When he left each city, it had become a model for new urbanism.

For example, when he went to Portsmouth as city manager, the downtown sported a cracked main street that hadn't been repaired since trolley tracks were pulled out decades earlier. Hanbury saw beyond the deteriorating infrastructure because he looked backward and forward at the same time.

We had a beautiful little historical district that was built in the eighteenth and early nineteenth centuries. We had the Customs House and the first naval hospital built in this country. I thought it was a beautiful historic district that had kind of gone to pot.

So I recommended that we invest in public improvements and then people would want to come over and see it. Where the dilapidated and vacant stores are, let's give the owners an incentive to use their store fronts and give them low-interest loans to remove the '50s and '60s facades and restore them to their historic beauty. Let's narrow the road, put in an attractive median with flowers and have brick sidewalks and gas lanterns.

We went with that, and Portsmouth became an historic area. Then new investment came in, and younger couples moved in, and the city prospered.

When Hanbury arrived in Fort Lauderdale in 1991, with decades of experience as city manager in Portsmouth and Virginia Beach, and assistant city manager in Norfolk and Virginia Beach, he had a track record of facing enormous urban challenges and transforming struggling cities into viable, healthy communities.

Fort Lauderdale was not without a vision. In 1984, the city held a referendum and went through some strategic planning exercises with the city commission, setting a goal to be the best city of its size by 1994. The city wanted to transform itself from a run-down spring-break town. The problem was one of execution. Although the downtown had been cleared of old buildings and there was a plan to develop shops and restaurants to exploit the city's river and canal system, very little had been done to transform the city from its dilapidated state in the six intervening years. Hanbury describes his first visit:

There had been no new residential projects built in downtown in over thirty-five years. There had been no new hotels built on Fort Lauderdale beach in over twenty years. All of the hotels were primarily used for spring break. Spring break was good for a three-month period. After that, it was rooms rented by the hour and that sort of thing. There wasn't much incentive to fix up what the spring breakers tore up. So, over a twenty-year period, the beach had deteriorated. There was no walkway, no bike trail, and people parked right on the beach. As I walked around the neighborhood near the beach, there were discarded needles and trash, and I was even propositioned in the middle of the tour!

Another potential city manager might have gone elsewhere quickly. But Hanbury enjoyed a challenge. He took the job because he believed he could not quit what he had started. It was a value instilled in him by his hardworking parents. As he looked around the tacky, tawdry beach landscape, he had a vision.

It went beyond the Riverwalk retail and entertainment development envisioned by the city leaders. He saw the transformation of Las Olas Boulevard, a four-lane state highway lined with shops that closed at five o'clock, to a thriving street of cafes where people dined *al fresco*, parked in front of the restaurants, enjoyed music, shopping, and entertainment, where streets bustled well into the night, and no one could distinguish the tourist season from the rest of the year.

I saw that it had tremendous potential. Contrary to all of the core cities I'd been in, Fort Lauderdale had all those canals and had kept its middle class. I saw the canals and the water and the ocean – after all, the good Lord wasn't making that kind of property any more. I thought it was a wonderful opportunity. We could have a viable, active downtown where people would want to live, shop, and work. The mayor, Bob Cox, said, 'George, we've been planning for years and it's time we did something. We keep planning and planning and nobody can get it done.'

Hanbury got it done. Like James Madison and the constitutional framers, Hanbury was ready to step up to a daunting challenge. Like the framers, he passed every decision through the prism of vision. He added his ideas to that of the citizens and slowly, a block at a time, propelled the city into fulfilling its promise and being recognized with a 'best city' award.

By the time he left the city manager's job eight years later, the modern Fort Lauderdale had risen by the ocean. Gleaming office towers, modern condos, and new hotels caught the breezes. The beach's signature was a lighted concrete wave wall. Revitalized neighborhoods lined the canals, new businesses thrived, and the Riverwalk and Las Olas shopping and entertainment districts pulsed with life late into the night.

Hanbury had major opposition and setbacks. When he arrived in Fort Lauderdale and began discussing his vision and what it would take to make it happen, he encountered strong opposition from the police and fire departments, because he asked their unions for concessions.

> It was none too pleasant. They were very upset with me. They wanted to fire me. They had posters and billboards and even planes flying over the stadium with the message, 'Save Fort Lauderdale, Fire Hanbury.'

> That impasse went on for about three years. I wouldn't agree to what they wanted, but I told them the same thing I had said in Portsmouth, 'If you help me, some of these things will be implemented, and then I can help you.'

> As the improvements happened, property values would rise and we could pay the police and firefighters. After about four or five years, it worked. When I left, the police honored me. They said, 'We didn't trust you. You were the new guy coming in here and we knew we could

outlast you, but what you said *was* true.' You have to convince people that there is something in the situation to benefit them.

Hanbury, like Alexander Hamilton and James Madison lobbying for ratification in *The Federalist* or arguing in their state constitutional ratifying conventions, kept the vision alive until enough people shared it and made it happen. He talked with civic associations and block committees, city workers and union leaders, commissioners and citizens. Like Madison, Hanbury excelled at the art of bringing individuals and groups to a point where they came to consensus and shared his vision.

Hanbury's doctoral work at nearby Florida Atlantic University sent him back to look at the work of the founding fathers. He became excited about Jefferson's intention to create an "academical village," a campus where theory and practice could blend. It takes a visionary to look at a 1970s shopping center and wasteland of abandoned parking lots and see a revolutionary new community combining commercial space, state-of-the-art research facilities, living and recreational space, and college classrooms. Yet that's what he saw at the fledgling Nova Southeastern University.

> When I came to Nova University in 1998, it just seemed like a natural that what Jefferson was professing, his concept of the 'academical village,' was probably the first mixed-used project ever. He wanted to have residential, commercial, retail, everything, so the students could see theory in practice. You read books about the new urbanism today, but Jefferson was trying to take urban Europe and put it right on the mountaintop in Virginia.

Jefferson wanted students to appreciate how theory

was supportive of practice, and without practice, the theory was no more than an exercise. Practice without theory would just remain stagnant and there would be no expansion.

I thought if we wrapped the buildings around the parking decks, and then make it an attractive area for people who want to live and work and do research, and then connect all of that to a doctoral research university with high-speed connections that tied into all other research universities in the state, you'd have quite an economic engine.

That's what I proposed, and the town of Davie agreed, and so we changed the zoning code.

Hanbury's casual reference to changing the zoning code illustrates another example of combing theory and practice in translating vision to reality. Changing zoning codes requires intricate legal and political steps. It's never easy, but to an experienced city manager, it's just another set of tasks.

Like Madison, Hanbury was experienced at getting people to act, knew how to compromise and make or broker a deal, and used political acumen to get results.

The Vision of Economic Engines

Hanbury's vision for Nova Southeastern University is not finished.

We will have three million square feet of research offices, residential, retail, a teaching hospital, a three-hundred-fifty-room hotel, a conference center, all interconnected to the university by a trolley system or rail and hopefully, someday we'll have that connection into mass transit.

You have all of the components of new urbanism; a university setting and a doctoral research program with a teaching hospital, and then you add in the collaborative research center where we'll be studying multiple diseases and their cures. So, it's an economic engine.

Hanbury is not the only former public official with the vision of a university as an economic engine. Donna Shalala has a similar vision for the University of Miami. When she arrived at the university in 2001, after serving eight years as Secretary of Health and Human Services in the Clinton administration, she was returning to academic work. She had served as president of Hunter College of the City University of New York and chancellor of the University of Wisconsin-Madison.

I've spent a career going in and out of the academy and government. Government gave me insights, because we are very much influenced by student aid, research dollars, and government regulations. That experience in complex public and private institutions served me well.

When I came to the University of Miami, I realized that we needed to get better and get better quickly. The university is really a national university, not a local one, and Florida deserves a world-class national university. But I also see our role as being an economic engine for our community, creating thousands of high-quality jobs.

We're not going to attract heavy industry to South Florida. We can attract health- and science-related jobs and the kinds of industries and businesses that are related to them. We can spin off ideas that create companies. I see us as very entrepreneurial, very much focused on the biomedical sciences and creating those kinds of high-quality jobs for our community. Many students who come here from the heartland want to stay here, and unless there are those great jobs, they're not going to stay.

So we're making a billion-dollar investment in our medical school and its research. We're building a new hospital, and we've just completed 350,000 square feet of research facilities. We're beefing up our professional schools in communications, business, education, and engineering, because that's where the new workforce is going to be trained.

Shalala has taken her extensive background in health care and applied that to guiding investments where they make a difference. She's overseen many building projects and brings that experience to the table, as well as her ability to manage a large, complex institution.

The success of Shalala's vision rested on procuring funding to improve academic ranking, research, and facilities. In launching a fund-raising campaign in 2001, she set her sights on bringing in $1 billion. A recent newspaper story tells the result:

UM Funding Drive Nets a Record $1.4 Billion

UM concluded its seven-year fundraising campaign with a record breaking $1.4 billion in donations and a boost to its national standing.[1]

As Shalala told a reporter, "No one in Florida had ever tried to raise this kind of money before...A lot of people thought we were nuts." Like anyone with a strong vision for the future, Shalala sees this as just the beginning of the continuing effort "specifically designed to propel UM up in national academic rankings." The money and rise in the standings go hand in hand, feeding one another. The money will "endow thirty-five new faculty chairs, construct or improve thirty-three buildings and provide more scholarships." One of the largest donations was from the Diabetes Research Institute Foundation for $80 million to support pioneering research at UM's Miller School of Medicine.

In her seven-year tenure, UM rose to fifty-second place in national academic rankings, one of two Florida schools in the top 100. It is more academically competitive, as demonstrated by the increasing SAT scores and higher grade point averages for incoming freshmen. As she told *The Miami Herald*, "We could not raise money if we were declining in the academic rankings. We could not raise money if we weren't getting better academically. So everything had to move together."[2]

Shalala also understands the necessity for a university to create a positive relationship with the community. As she quips, "Universities are universities, but the context in Miami gives it a special kind of twist." She's referring to the multicultural community's close connections to Latin America and the Caribbean, a population in transition from retirees to young families, and a business community working to move from a primary focus on tourism to more medical and biotech research.

Shalala's government experience gives her "access to Congress and to agencies, and I know how they work and how they think." In singling out Thomas Jefferson as her favorite founder, she says, "He was a Renaissance man. He was as interested in planning out a campus as he was participating in arguments about freedom."

While Jefferson was not at the Constitutional Convention (he was in Paris serving as ambassador), he was keenly interested in what was going on. Despite the ocean separating Jefferson and Madison, they kept up their correspondence. Jefferson had firm views on what the new constitution should contain and he shared them readily with Madison. He wanted to make sure *his* vision of the future United States became a reality.

Vision also was the driving force when John Stunson took

over as city manager in Oakland Park, Florida in 2001. It was a city in crisis. Many executives in this position would simply roll up their sleeves and do what needed to be done in the short term to rectify the situation. There didn't seem to be breathing space to think about a future vision for the city. Stunson realized that he had to do both. He had a head start because he had managed the city previously, from 1974-1983.

Historically, the relationship between city government and the residents was often stormy. Oakland Park was a small city stretched along the railroad tracks. Its population was mostly working-class renters, not home owners. The city was in a major financial crisis in 2001 when Stunson returned. "When I looked over the annual audit, the city had spent most of its reserves and I understood if we didn't do something, we would not make the budget and we'd be in serious trouble in six months." The city also incurred a large debt from former redevelopment efforts, so the picture was bleak.

Stunson took the painful action of reducing the workforce by about five percent and changing the fee structures and *ad valorem* taxes. Like all good executives, he knew he couldn't cut his way to success, so he brought in new finance and human resources directors who could help build the "bench strength to help the rest of the changes we needed to make." Midway through the changes, three hurricanes caused major flooding in the city, which sits only five feet above sea level. Luckily, money was available for flood mitigation from the Federal Emergency Management Agency. Now the city could rectify the problems caused by earlier reconstruction projects which exacerbated the flooding.

Stunson wasn't content to dive into just the immediate problems of the city. He had a vision. He saw a prosperous, thriving city with a sustainable tax base that would be a pleasant place to live. He set about transforming the culture of both Oakland Park and the city government to make his vision a reality. His culture change initiative is succeeding.

Hanbury, Shalala, and Stunson are similar to delegates to

the Constitutional Convention who had been in public life and were politically savvy. Michael Howe resembles those framers who came from the arena of business and commerce, yet who also knew how to translate vision into reality.

Michael Howe was not an obvious candidate to take on the vision of transforming health care. "I was selling toothpaste and deodorant at Proctor & Gamble and I was selling roast beef sandwiches at Arby's," he says. As an executive with P&G, and later PepsiCo and KFC, he was recognized as a talented leader. He wanted the opportunity to run a company, and that came when Arby's offered him a job running about one-third of the operation. "They were trying to recreate the environment. I thought, 'Boy, that sounds exciting.'" Within a few years, he was CEO of the entire company, set about creating a new vision, and ultimately transformed Arby's.

Part of that transformation was to move from an employer to a franchise-based company. In the process, Arby's would shrink from nine thousand employees to just one hundred thirty. After everyone was informed of the change, Howe brought in people from across the company, including some who were losing their jobs, to discuss how to change the culture. They helped him put together a prioritized culture-change plan focused on recognition, career advancement, and communication.

One day he got a call from a director of MinuteClinic, a CVS Caremark Corporation subsidiary. It operates drop-in, non-critical, quick health-care facilities in some CVS pharmacies. The clinics are generally staffed by physicians' assistants and nurse practitioners who can diagnose and treat a specified list of common health problems and simple, urgent needs. When Howe went to his first interview, he remarked, "I really appreciate meeting you, but somebody screwed up and misread my resume. I have no health-care experience. I can't help you guys!" The director replied, "That's exactly why we want you!" Howe was intrigued — and hooked. He took the job as CEO.

Much like the framers at the Constitutional Convention, Howe was stepping up to do something groundbreaking. Although some framers had developed their states' constitutions, none had ever taken on a task as enormous as transforming a national government. Howe tells how he took on the challenge of health care.

> Over breakfast, the CVS executives taught me a lot about health care. I came here to Minnesota [MinuteClinic's headquarters] because it was an opportunity to do something significant. There are so few times in your life that you're presented with a wonderful business opportunity that has societal value.
>
> The vision is really about fundamentally changing health-care delivery. It's an intersection of retail and health care. I visualize it as two streets coming together and you need to stand on all four corners to see it completely. You need the science and art of health care and you need the service and art of retail to make this concept work.

Ben Baldanza is another visionary who wants to transform an industry. He studied transportation economics in graduate school, and was fascinated with the airline business. His is a unique perspective.

> People don't fly because the want to. They fly because they're going to do something else; go on vacation, or a business trip, or visit relatives. Every minute you're in an airport or an airplane is an intermediate good. You don't buy it for what it is, but to help you with something else.
>
> How do you take an intermediate good and make it something relevant to customers and help customers actually enjoy the experience — even though they don't

want to be there?

After years in the industry at carriers large and small, Baldanza, CEO of Spirit Airlines, has a vision based on this idea of transforming the experience for the customer. He wanted the low-cost carrier to be the largest international airline flying out of Fort Lauderdale-Hollywood International Airport. He focused on the Caribbean and Latin American markets, leveraging the increasing population in South Florida from these areas, to build Spirit to be the seventh-busiest carrier in South Florida. "As we look at it, the Fort Lauderdale airport is not just a low-fare alternative to Miami. It's a legitimate gateway. We were the first to have this vision and now we're building that gateway." To make his vision a reality, Baldanza started building a different company culture.

Create a Culture

Vision becomes reality, according to the interviewed leaders, by creating a culture that supports the vision. The framers of the Constitution and the founders of the Republic shared a common vision of a society where "to secure these Rights, [Life, Liberty, and the Pursuit of Happiness] Governments are instituted among Men, deriving their just Powers from the Consent of the Governed."

During the Constitutional Convention, the framers made several decisions to shape a new culture based on the consent of the governed. The new government's structure would be different from the colonial and state governments it was supplanting. For example, they rejected property qualifications for all offices and representatives. Over the next decade, most states also lifted these restrictions. In fact, many of the Constitution ratifying conventions were the most democratic bodies elected up to that point.[3]

They rejected proposals to distinguish between the rights of the original thirteen states and new states; require religious tests for office holders and representatives; and impose onerous barriers for immigrants who wanted to become citizens. With the exception of the presidency, they allowed naturalized citizens to hold all offices. The framers forbade titles of nobility and rejected sumptuary laws that would have forbidden ostentatious dress. They accepted two-year terms for the people's body, the House of Representatives, to assure regular involvement by citizens. They provided six-year terms for senators (initially appointed by the states) to ensure continuity and restrain hasty decisions. They provided four-year terms for the executive office, the presidency, and hoped to prevent aristocracy and monarchy from creeping back in, although they did not limit the number of terms a person served.

Culture Wars

Unfortunately, within a few years, the new national leaders quickly parted company as they attempted to define the broader *culture* that would achieve their vision.

Thomas Jefferson, and those who joined his faction, believed that to maintain virtue among the people to sustain a republic, the society should be agriculturally based. Trade in agricultural goods would provide the revenue for a minimal federal government, and most power should reside in the states.

Hamilton and his faction saw a very different path to the Revolutionary vision. They saw the development of businesses of all kinds, manufacturing and industry, stocks and finance, as the only way to build a strong central government that could promote international trade, as well as a permanent army that could stave off enemies.

The early years of the republic were dominated by the monumental battles between these two equally visionary groups. Each emerging political party believed its road to the American vision was the *only* one that would work. Their high rhetoric and low skullduggery was our first culture war as a nation. As Jefferson's Republican Party[4] fought Hamilton's

Federalists[5] for the soul of the nation, ideologues in both camps believed the others were traitors who were destroying the republic.

The presidential campaign of 1800 pitted Vice President Thomas Jefferson against President John Adams, and it was one of the dirtiest in our history. Each side outdid the other in manipulating public opinion and the media, creating vile rumors and innuendo, and indulging in unbridled mudslinging and lies to destroy the credibility of the other.[6] After losing the bitter campaign, Adams, who was accused of packing the judiciary, left town in the middle of the night so he would not have to witness Jefferson's inauguration.

As soon as Jefferson was ensconced in office, he tried to undo all the Adams' judicial appointments and created confrontations with the Supreme Court, which was headed by his hated cousin John Marshall, a Federalist. Ironically, these confrontations led to rulings that firmly established the Court as the final arbiter of our laws and the Constitution.

Jefferson and Adams, once close comrades in the Continental Congress during the Revolution, and members of the committee charged with writing the Declaration of Independence, remained estranged for years. Finally, aided by a mutual friend, they began corresponding in their final years, renewing their fond friendship and giving modern readers an insight into the minds of two of our most important founders. They both died on the same Fourth of July, exactly 50 years after the Declaration was signed. Neither could have engineered a more dramatic, symbolic departure.

Although these two leaders reconciled, the country did not. America continued along several different paths toward the republican vision. Some of those fault lines led to attempts by various groups of states to break away from the Union and form their own separate confederations, perhaps allied with other nations. The final rupture came in 1861, as the South attempted to break away from the Union. The failure to create a unifying culture was one of the fault lines in American society that led to the devastating carnage and destruction wrought by the Civil War. These same fault lines continue to splinter the nation. The culture wars continue, as modern political parties try to define what our values are and how we will reach the vision stated in the Declaration of Independence. The founders' vision remains a counter and unifying force, but their dream of a common path to that vision has not been fulfilled.

The Hard Job of Building a Culture

Building a new culture is not an easy task. In fact, the odds are stacked against it. Case studies of companies' attempts to build new cultures abound. Typically, new leaders make bold statements about the cultural transformation they will achieve. A flurry of activity follows. Eventually, the ideas of the new culture succumb to the powerful inertia of the old. In the worst failures, the new culture's ideas and catch phrases become jokes that feed cynicism and make future change efforts even more difficult.

A minority of leaders do build new cultures. The common denominator is this: the leaders start with a vision and relentlessly share that vision with every employee until the critical mass embraces the new culture and agrees to pursue the vision.

The framers at the Constitutional Convention weren't just trying to create a new culture by embedding their beliefs about human society in government infrastructure. Many were committed to continuing in public life, even at great personal sacrifice, to make the vision a reality. Through voluminous public and private writing, support or opposition to legislation, they kept chipping away at the old colonial cultures of the states, trying to establish their version of the new American culture.

Howard Putnam, Southwest Airlines' former CEO, understood this grassroots strategy of how to build a new culture. "Probably forty percent of my time the first year, I was out doing nothing but pounding the vision into the organization; one-on-one, one-on-two, one-on-three. Everyone understood exactly what kind of business we were in."

Gregory Swienton came to Ryder System as president and COO in 1999. When he became CEO in 2000, he realized his real agenda was culture change. Charged with revitalizing the company and facing the typical challenges of cutting costs and tightening processes, he wanted to do more and transform the culture. He envisioned a company that would be

> ...recognized as a consistent performer, a company that provided exceptional performance for shareholders, and a company that employees are really proud to be part of, and where customers seek our solutions. It's also got to be a company that's supportive of the environment. We have to deliver to all those constituencies.
>
> It's the values and the culture that support the fact that you want to perform well. You want to deliver the best in good times and in bad. We have twenty-seven thousand people, and no matter what I think or what a leadership team thinks, we need everyone on the same consistent path. It's similar to the framers. You've got very bright people with very good intentions and very diverse opinions. So the key is to articulate the vision in a simple, clear way. Things don't have to be complicated. You want to communicate certain messages in as simple and articulate a way as possible, so everyone eventually hears exactly the same thing.
>
> It's a constant effort. My favorite part of the job now is to meet with customers and with employees. We talk directly, in town meetings or across the table. But we have written statements and videos and even audio tapes for our drivers on the road. So I try never to get

off message, even if I'm tired of saying it. It might be the first time the person is hearing it. That's how you change the culture.

John Zumwalt made creating a new culture the hallmark of his term as CEO of PBS&J. Because of his thirty-plus years there, he knew the founders and admired their strong values. "You could see the values of the firm walking down the hall every day," he said. When he became CEO, Zumwalt realized he had to make some changes to the culture to incorporate the values of the founders with the need for more policies and processes. He wanted to recapture what was positive about the original culture.

> I'm promoting a culture of leadership and values, and underneath that, change. I think the tone is set at the top. If I'm doing it and people around me are doing it, we create an atmosphere where people aren't afraid to talk. I think about Washington. He certainly set the tone and people perceived him to be righteous.

Michael Howe's first attempt at corporate culture change got off to a rocky start. As he began his leadership at Arby's, he realized the company needed more than better bottom-line results. It needed a new culture to get those results. He proposed the leadership team develop a strategic plan for the culture, as well as the business.

> My staff laughed me out of the room. I started talking culture to the directors. At first, I wasn't too successful. But I kept talking about how we had to make it a better place to work. I kept getting the 'huh?' look, but I kept on talking about it.

> I kept on working on the culture and we started getting some terrific results. We took the cash flow from the

business from about $36 million to $65 million in a little over four years, and at the same time, we grew sales about ten or twelve percent.

We got those results because the organization really understood how to maximize the resources it had. And that came out of the culture that came out of people wanting to do it. The basic change I made was to open up communication. To me, leadership needs to be situational and more egalitarian.

I would welcome new people to the company and talk about it a little and then ask them a question, 'Why do you get a paycheck?' I'd get the usual answers, some of them quite interesting. Then I'd say, 'In my estimation, you're given a paycheck for one reason, and that's to exercise your judgment.'

I told them, 'You're unique. You have a responsibility to use the gifts that you bring to the organization. So if something isn't right, I expect you to raise your hand and say so. If you're not using your judgment, you're not earning your paycheck.' And they stepped up. The culture changed, and results followed.

At MinuteClinic, Howe took a similar approach.

We're growing rapidly, and our challenge is keeping the vision clear. In training new employees and managers, we've built that in. We talk about the vision and their role in fulfilling it. We spend a day and a half of the week-long orientation working on the culture; what it is, what we're trying to create, what their roles are, what the behaviors are that we want them to embrace.

> When we went through our JCAHO [Joint Commission on Accreditation of Healthcare Organizations] accreditation, the observer pointed out how consistently everyone was able to verbalize the vision and mission and how consistent we were about what we were trying to accomplish. The team has done a great job of really embracing what we're trying to do, and it shows up in the interviews with our staff that appear in the press.

Howe's vision is paying off. Although he later left MinuteClinic, President George W. Bush had appointed him to a commission studying the future of health care and has consulted with him directly.[7]

For Ben Baldanza, changing the culture at Spirit Airlines was crucial. He began by turning hiring on its head.

> Traditionally, Spirit hired for competence and specific experience, like most companies. So we hired flight attendants, gate agents, and reservations people who had the competencies for those particular jobs. That sounds like a good thing. Without trivializing those jobs, the reality is that we can train people to be effective and competent in those jobs. What we can't train is how to smile well, what we call the 'natural tendency to like people.' So today we hire for that talent. We hire smart, because we're about becoming a 'good service' airline.

> I'm building a different culture here at Spirit. I keep an open mind. No one has a monopoly on good ideas. I've created forums for communication and opportunities for people to share ideas. I'm going out to the airport in a little while to talk to flight attendants as the planes come in. I don't have any agenda. I don't have any slides to show them. It's just to hear what they've been seeing. I get out on the road and talk to employees a lot. Of course, we have formal feedback through the web

and e-mail, and we follow up on what employees tell us. They all have my personal internal e-mail address and they know I'll respond.

In the city of Oakland Park, City Manager John Stunson began his culture change efforts by solving the problem of animosity between community organizations and city government. He realized he must strengthen community leadership. He established the Leadership Academy to train community activists.

In our last class, fifty percent of the people either became executives of community associations or part of the city boards. We've even hired a few of them. Now we're going to the next stage after stabilizing everything. We are linked to the community through the Managers Round Table. It's made up of people who graduated from the Leadership Academy, or who are association presidents, or sit on community boards. This way we have broad input, because everyone is interested in the city's redevelopment.

Stunson's efforts of inclusion and civic education for people who previously led vocal protests and opposition to city government harnessed that energy for culture change. The results were not unlike what happened in the colonies in the lead-up to and aftermath of the Revolution. Despite the elite status of the framers, most would not have qualified for their positions and professions in British society. Some of the Convention delegates came from very humble origins. Even Washington was denied appropriate rank in the British army during colonial times because he lacked high social status. Although some founding fathers decried the so-called "leveling spirit" of the Revolution, they were part of it. They also set the stage for even more leveling by removing property as a requirement for suffrage and holding office.

Stunson followed the same concept in Oakland Park, helping working-class people, some with little formal education, move into leadership positions to improve their community and enhance their street-smart organizing skills. As he reports,

> What we've focused on is trying to build the cadre of leadership that's needed to change the culture. We get ideas from the citizens and the workers, and then move it up the chain. That's challenging *in* our culture and *to* our culture. When there's conflict — and any time you want to do something in a city, there's some conflict — I get people around a table and we talk through the issues.

Stunson also adapted the continuous improvement philosophy of Dr. W. Edwards Deming to renew the city's culture.

> We've created a Performance Excellence Initiative based on the Baldrige and Sterling processes for improving quality.[8] We brought in someone who worked with another city to gain the Sterling award. Our public works director has become a certified Sterling examiner, so we can really understand what we need to do to continuously improve our city and its services.

Stunson brought in two local, high-profile, experienced leaders to conduct retreats that bring the city commissioners, community, and city leaders together to tackle the biggest issues. To solve his need for a sustainable tax-base, Stunson led an annexation effort that brought in an adjacent community of ten thousand home owners who also are changing the city's culture.

> We're also changing the culture with our values. We've worked to bring on people with a desire for public service. We had to work on respect and integrity for

a long time. Every one of our senior people has been through training and mentoring, and we measure their progress. It comes down to basic trust.

George Hanbury also knows something about how to change a culture. He took his successful formula for changing cities and followed it at Nova Southeastern University.

One thing I learned from my experience as a city manager is, you don't convince elected officials, the general public, your partners, trustees, or faculty by just expressing your vision verbally. Most people need to see something so they can digest it.

So, the first thing I did was get a land-use planner and an architect and then we were able to show visuals — how this academical village idea would work; how it would look; how tall the buildings would be; how it would impact the residential community surrounding it. By doing all of that, I had no opposition.

I went out to meetings with the citizens and neighborhood organizations. Sometimes I had to sit up until eleven or twelve o'clock at night. But when the plan did come up for rezoning, I actually had some people in the residential neighborhood who waited that late to encourage the town council to vote for it.

Vision Needs Culture

Executing vision requires a nurturing culture. Building that culture is the job of the leader. George Washington was acutely aware of his influence on the culture he was creating within the new government as its first executive. Modern scholars acknowledge the debt we owe him in making the vision of republican government a reality. He thought through every aspect of his behavior, as well as his decisions.

Modern scholars[10] document how Washington, from an early age, consciously molded his public character. As the first President of the Republic, he knew he had a huge responsibility to set the tone and strike the right note as an executive. He already had shown what a republican military leader does when he resigned his army commission at the end of the Revolution, and returned to managing his properties as a private citizen.

He studiously avoided tipping his hand during the Constitutional Convention, lest his iconic status stifle debate. In fact, on the last day, when he suggested changing the number of people represented in Congressional districts, everyone immediately agreed without discussion.

Washington thought through every public action and asked the counsel of trusted advisors on how to behave and what to say as well as on important national policy matters. He knew he was the role model others would follow. Finally, at the end of his second term as president, Washington passed the reins of government and power to an elected successor. At the time, there were still those who would have made him the elected king for life. Washington would have none of it. Even King George III in England acknowledged Washington's greatness in giving up power through the electoral process.

But even Washington failed at developing a high-performing executive team. His first cabinet was certainly made up of proven leaders — Thomas Jefferson as Secretary of State, General George Knox as Secretary of War, and Alexander Hamilton as Secretary of the Treasury. As already discussed, Jefferson and Hamilton had their own agendas for creating a new culture. Neither was entirely in alignment with Washington. Hamilton favored an even stronger executive branch and supported the idea of a president elected for life. Jefferson stood at the opposite end of the spectrum and preferred a weaker national government and presidency. Not long after Jefferson took up his post, he began to organize his faction into a political party.

The acrimony between Hamilton and Jefferson, two titans of the Revolution, became more and more personal and spilled over into the cabinet. Washington became angry and frustrated as he found himself, after all his prodigious leadership triumphs, unable to get these two men to work as a team.

Although none of the modern leaders interviewed faced a challenge as impossible as trying to reconcile Jefferson and Hamilton, they did have to work hard to build their teams and create a common culture. Remember Michael Howe as he tried to introduce culture change to his Arby's team?

Even Washington could not go it alone. Strong leaders need strong teams. Washington's team was merely headstrong. After Jefferson resigned from the Cabinet, Hamilton and the Federalists pushed their agenda forward. When Jefferson returned in triumph as president in 1800, he set about undoing the Federalist culture and trying to establish his own party's culture as the dominant force in American life.

Make the Vision Real

The modern leaders tell the same story. First they articulated a vision. Then they talked to people inside the company and in the community, no matter how many people or how scattered geographically. They engaged individuals and talked about their vision. They listened to people and established various ways to continue getting truth from the trenches. The roadmap to building a culture to reach the vision is as simple, and as difficult, as that.

The difference between visionaries and visionary leaders is this: Visionary leaders share their vision, one-on-one. That intimate dialogue converts employees and managers into a team heading in one direction, engaged and taking action to translate the vision into reality. The prescription is simple, yet hard to execute. Have a vision. Convey that vision consistently and persistently to everyone. Build a culture, person by person, that will support the vision and nurture it every step of the way.

But a vision of the future is not enough to get you there. Even a transformed culture is not enough. Everything may still be too abstract. Successful leaders need another powerful strategy for moving into their desired future. They have to answer one defining question: What do I need to do to get people mobilized and moving forward Monday morning, and every day after that?

Article III

Get People on a Mission

"If you get people on a mission, metrics will follow."
— John Zumwalt, CEO, PBSJ Corporation

As inspired as the Revolutionary Generation of the late 1700s was by the long-term ideal of an American republic where "all men are created equal," they knew it would take more than vision to make things happen. They understood the importance of a concrete mission. In the final days of the Constitutional Convention, the framers created one last committee to shape the language in their document. Much of that work fell to Gouverneur Morris.[1]

Morris came from a prominent and wealthy New York family. Despite his aristocratic origins, he believed in the republican cause, and was active in the Convention and during the Revolution, although no one would accuse him of being a 'democrat.' In fact, he strongly opposed the leveling spirit of the faction that eventually coalesced around Thomas Jefferson. Still, he had a strong belief in the work of the Constitutional Convention, and is the one person responsible for turning the turbulent, messy, confusing mass of decisions into the compact, clear, no-nonsense prose we appreciate today. Morris also took one more critical step. Drawing variously on the Articles of Confederation, a variety of state constitutions, and well-known Enlightenment sources of the time, he crafted a preamble for the new Constitution. It is the embodiment of a perfect mission statement.

We the People of the United States,
in Order to form a more perfect Union,
establish Justice,
insure domestic Tranquility,
provide for the common defense,
promote the general Welfare, and
secure the Blessings of Liberty to ourselves and our Posterity,
do ordain and establish this Constitution for the United States of America.

This statement does exactly what a good mission should do: it tells us what we are going to do, why we're going to do it, and who is going to do what for whom.

Fifty-two words. No overblown marketing hype or meaningless corporate jargon; just a simple statement of fact that can be understood by everyone. When the mission statement is this clear, it binds the individual to the organization and becomes a powerful tool for daily action and decision making.

Mission Drives Strategic Action

When the mission is so clear and concise, it empowers individuals to easily act strategically at every level of the organization. They only have to ask themselves one simple question: "Is this action or decision leading me closer to or further from accomplishing my mission?" The dilemma for leaders is how to get everyone to ask this crucial question.

To discover the secret of modern mission-making, imagine being in the beautifully restored, bustling historic district of Portsmouth, Virginia a few years ago. City workers from every department mill around with citizens, tourists, and officials, all waiting expectantly for the guest of honor. Finally, he appears and stands under the banner declaring "George Hanbury Day." Hanbury walks across the platform and addresses the assembly — eighteen years *after* he left his position as city manager. Why did the current city manager, former members of the city council, current department heads, and long-time employees flock to hear Hanbury?

A former garbage collector who was there that day summed up the reasons when he told Hanbury, "I still remember to this day: 'Clean City, Economic Development, and Customer Service.' " Decades after the city had morphed from a down-at-the-heels, decaying relic into a thriving community, a worker who was part of that transformation could still recite the mission. Hanbury knows how to bind everyone to the mission to get results. As he said,

> What I did was to try to get buy-in throughout the organization that, regardless of your job, you had a major role in one of those three areas of the mission. If we had a clean city, we were going to generate economic development. If we were customer-service oriented, we would have the other two aspects. Simple. I told people, if we did those three things, we'd solve the problems of the city and people could start getting pay raises again.
>
> Portsmouth developed its historic area and now all the stuff I talked about, new investment and people coming in, happened. But it took a lot of hard work and good leadership to convince the citizens and city workers, because they were looking at the city like an armpit. But I would say, 'If you work with me, I'll work with you.' As the city improved, I could get them the raises they wanted.

John Zumwalt also understands the importance of a strong mission in transforming an organization. When Zumwalt moved into the corner office at PBS&J, he had some formidable challenges. The founders of the engineering services company were survivors of the Great Depression and World War

II. Zumwalt admired these leaders and he translated that admiration into action.

> To me, the Greatest Generation was a leadership generation. They had the country on a mission. You had [President John F.] Kennedy saying, 'Let's put a man on the moon and bring him back safely.'[2] You had [President Ronald] Reagan saying, 'Mr. Gorbachev, tear down that wall.' Leaders are on missions. Managers love their metrics.
>
> The framers of the Constitution all had different agendas. It was the same here at PBS&J. How do you get them on the same page? You have a truly compelling mission that sits deep within your values and culture and you move on it. The real question is, 'how do we capture the heart?' We know how to capture the mind, but how do you put the heart into moving the agenda?

Mission Drives Success

Zumwalt's belief in the power of the mission as the internal driver of success has been put to the test many times. During his tenure as COO, he realized that PBS&J needed to consolidate several acquired companies into one coherent organization. To overcome the difficulties inherent in so many separate cultures, Zumwalt told the board, "Let's give the consolidated company a single mission and have a single purpose for everybody." The reason? "Our overall mission was 'to become nationally recognized as the consultant of choice.' We knew to do that, we had to become the employer of choice."

When Zumwalt became president of PBS&J in 2000, the turnover rate was a little more than eighteen percent. When told that the industry turnover rate was twenty-two percent, he fired back, "Then the industry is screwed up!" It wasn't just a matter of hiring the top talent; he also needed to get them to stay. Zumwalt believed he also needed to look at more than engineering talent. He began looking for people who could "bring a passion for their work that would be noticed by their clients." He wanted people who cared as much about people as they did about engineering.

He believes one of the keys was inculcating leadership as a central theme for all managers. He emphasizes leadership with all of his managers and constantly engages them. "I know what your metrics are. What's your mission? It's not about making metrics. *If you get people on a mission, metrics will follow.*" He started Leadership PBS&J, a program that has developed such a positive reputation that people from outside beg to join it, even though the program is only open to employees. By 2006, turnover was at nine percent, and the company's key metrics soared.

Today, Zumwalt faces a new challenge in driving his company to accomplish the mission. A new generation, the GenYs, also known as the Millennials, are coming into the workforce, joining the GenXers. It is a generation quite different from the Boomers, who tend to dominate management positions.

> We actually looked at the twenty-and thirty-somethings together. We found out they didn't want to achieve like their parents, because they were the ones whose parents were working all the time and didn't attend their ball games and school plays. But they did want to innovate. Of course, they wanted to make a salary, but they wanted to do something more. They wanted to innovate *and* have a cause. They wanted to do something for the society and the community where they lived and worked.
>
> For me, the challenge is now, 'How do you tap into that energy and bring it forward so they can continue to innovate, so they can stay passionate and not get

beaten down?' That's why leaders are on a mission and get their teams on a mission.

People on a Mission Get Better Results

Understanding the critical role that mission plays in getting results doesn't depend solely on the record of the Constitutional framers or on contemporary leaders' anecdotal evidence. In 1999, the Gallup organization released a groundbreaking study defining great managers, *First Break All the Rules*.[3] One of the critical elements for employees turned out to be, "The mission or purpose of my company makes me feel important." People who worked for the top-ranked managers strongly agreed with this statement.

Gallup followed their initial study in 2006 with even more substantial results from companies which had applied the lessons from the first book.[4] The Constitutional framers might have nodded with knowing approval. These are just a few of their findings about the criticality of mission in achieving results:[5]

- Eighty-three percent of all workers believed having a clear mission was very important;
- When companies were ranked by how strongly their employees agreed with the importance of mission, the top quartile had profitability that was from five percent to fifteen percent higher than the companies in the lowest quartile;
- Work groups with a clear sense of mission had from thirty percent to fifty percent fewer accidents; and,
- Mission-driven work groups had from fifteen to thirty percent less turnover.

The Gallup researchers concluded it was "as if *the employee can't energize himself to do all he could without knowing how his job fits into the grand scheme of things.*"[6]

The Gallup research provides some objective proof of what both the Constitution's framers and contemporary leaders discovered from experience: humans need a sense of daily purpose, a mission to motivate themselves to act and accomplish goals.

The Gallup work also found the influence of the leader is not as important in many areas as leaders would like to think, with one key exception: the mission. When the leader is on a mission, it cascades throughout the organization. The mission, however, can lose strength on the way down the organizational hierarchy unless the message is repeated and reinforced constantly. This constant reinforcement is exactly what leaders interviewed did. Remember the garbage collector in Portsmouth? Eighteen years later, he still remembered, cared about, and practiced the mission George Hanbury and others had repeated thousands of times. Sending out a memo just won't do the trick.

However, even a well-conceived mission can fail to get results. A case in point is a well-established company whose leadership team updated the mission statement. Afterward, one of the executives talked with every employee about it. The executive reinforced the importance of the mission by giving anyone who could repeat the vision and mission statement a reward token. The executive gave out lots of tokens; many people proudly displayed them. Yet, despite the 'success' of that campaign, nothing much changed. Why? No one with decision-making power talked about the new mission, or used it to make decisions, or followed it to take action. In fact, the managers and supervisors never mentioned the mission again. It joined thousands of other mission statements hanging on company walls — pretty plaques with no tangible results.

Think once again about the Portsmouth mission: "Clean City, Economic Development, and Customer Service." No matter what their function or level, city workers can look at everything they do within that context. A clerk in the buildings department can ask, "What am I doing to provide great customer service to the frustrated contractor at my desk trying to get a permit?" A garbage collector can ask, "Did I replace those trash cans neatly after I emptied them to ensure a clean city?" The finance director can ask, "Did I make a thorough study to find ways to provide incentives for business owners to fix up their property in order to spur economic development?"

The mission is where the hard work of translating ideas into reality starts. The payoff is in the results. Many companies blow the step from mission to result. How does an organization make that journey successfully?

Mission Drives Culture Drives Results

Alan Levine came to Broward Health after a successful stint as the Florida Secretary for Health Care Administration. Broward Health is one of the five largest not-for-profit public health-care systems in the U.S. and operates a number of large public hospitals and health-care facilities in the region around Fort Lauderdale. It had revenues of $1 billion in 2007, and serves a population diverse in age, ethnicity, and income, where twenty-four percent of patients are uninsured.

Shortly after Levine took the helm as CEO, he faced a major crisis. A patient who came into one of the hospitals for a minor reason died when given the wrong dose of a drug.

Levine didn't hesitate to stand up to the criticism immediately. He launched an investigation, called in the media, and explained the situation step by step. He made no excuses, nor did he try to cover up the story. His approach echoes that of other strong leaders. As he explains, "The key is to take an adverse incident like that and turn it into something that we can learn from so it doesn't happen again. Hopefully, other hospitals will learn from it and look at their processes."

Levine has a personal mission. He lost his mother when he was only six years old and vowed he would go into the medical field. With masters' degrees in health care and business administration, he took on a number of assignments in various institutions. He was COO of an HCA hospital,[7] ran a small rural hospital, served as former Florida Governor Jeb Bush's health-care advisor, and then as the state's Secretary for Health Care Administration.

When Levine began working with his leadership team at Broward Health, he discovered mission and vision statements that read like novels. "If it's not succinct, people are confused. We changed it so that everyone can understand it and buy in," he said. He realized his leadership team's priorities would be critical, and worked to build a culture where patient satisfaction would come first. His new mission points everyone in the new direction. "The mission of Broward Health is to be the regional leader, in partnership with and for the benefit of our community, in the provision of an integrated system of health-care services."

How does the mission specifically guide their decision making? Levine said the leadership team was working on a marketing plan when someone suggested an advertising campaign built around one of their premier programs, such as cancer care or surgery. Levine pointed out that their patient satisfaction ratings in the emergency room were low. "If our patient satisfaction is low, and we spend a few million on advertising and they all come here and have a bad experience, guess what? No, the first thing is to change the culture so that patient satisfaction is the most important thing."

Implementing the mission requires culture change, just like pursuing the vision. One of Levine's decisions was to change the name of the institution from the North Broward Hospital District to Broward Health, a name more reflective of the new mission and vision. Part of the vision statement reads, "The system will focus on optimizing the health status of our entire community through a complete continuum of services, including wellness initiatives." As he told a reporter, "A district's not where you want to bring you family [for health care.] It sounds like a police precinct."[8]

Levine never deviates from that message. He beams with

pleasure when he recounts a friend's experience in one of his facilities. He says she told him, "My experience was great. I had a nurse ask me, 'is there anything I can do to make you feel better?'" He continues,

> What better for a nurse to ask? That's the culture we want. We want a culture where they think critically and constantly ask, 'How can I make you feel better?' Once you've got everybody focused on that mission, everything flows from that. Then patients will be willing to come back, and you're building that loyalty. Then you can start talking to them about all the great things you do.
>
> Every week or two, I send out an e-mail to every employee and ask people to print them for people who don't have e-mail. Here's a typical response, 'Mr. Levine, thank you so much for sharing this. It's the first time anybody's told us what we're trying to do and what's going on.'
>
> With the state budget cuts and tax reform, we're going to have real challenges. I say, 'Here's what you can do to help.' If you get them engaged, they want to help. I expect my managers to carry the message, too.

Insuring the Mission to Get Results

Implementing the mission as a guide for decision making required more than staying on message for Levine. He looked at the incentive system in an effort to discover what was driving daily action and decision making. He found that managers were rewarded when they hit net income targets, were accredited by JCAHO,[9] and maintained an eighty percent patient satisfaction rate. Overall, these incentives resulted in stagnant operating performance.

Levine immediately saw that this system could not achieve

either the new vision or mission. First, net income included investment income and tax revenues. The latter had been driven by rising property taxes; neither element was under the control of the executives and managers. He removed these 'fudge factors' from the operating income targets.

Second, as he laid out bluntly to everyone, "I look at accreditation the opposite way. You get fired if you don't stay accredited. It's not something you get a bonus for. It's at the core of your job."

Levine calculated that an eighty percent patient satisfaction rate translated to below the seventieth percentile nationwide. In other words, patients in over thirty percent of U.S. hospitals were more satisfied with their care. During his first year, he set the target at a ninety percent patient satisfaction rate for both the ER and inpatient areas. The following year, he set the target at ninety-six percent patient satisfaction, aiming to be better than ninety percent of all U.S. hospitals. "It all starts with aligning the incentives with the vision and mission. People understand how important these are now, because the mission and vision are reflected in the incentive plan. People are buying in."

Accomplishing Broward Health's mission is still plagued by national policies that reimburse doctors by the number of days a patient stays in the hospital, yet only reimburse the hospitals a flat fee regardless of the length of the stay. Levine continues to stress improving the indicators that keep the daily focus on the patient experience. He knows the emphasis on patients will eventually lead to the recognition of Broward Health as one of the top health-care delivery systems in the nation – a core component of the vision statement.

Levine's focus on mission *has* gotten solid results. As reported in the media, Broward Health:

- Decreased reliance on property tax, down to fifteen percent of revenue, a major improvement — even as tax revenues plummeted due to tax reform in the state;[10]

- Increased the number of paying patients significantly;[11]
- Received an upgraded bond rating from Moody's Investment Services, who upped the rating to "A2". Standard & Poor's upgraded its rate to "A";[12]
- Allowed the board to cut the millage (tax) rate to its lowest in twenty-five years ;[13]
- Increased patient satisfaction at Broward General, a main hospital of Broward Health, from sixty-six percent to ninety-three percent;[14] and,
- Decreased expenses in two years by $30 million, with $50 million more in reductions projected over the next six years.[15]

Levine is the first to remind people that, "You can't just cut your way to success."[16] For example, when the staff at Broward General Hospital achieved that major improvement to ninety-three percent patient satisfaction, he made sure every non-management employee got a one-week bonus. In a letter to employees, Levine said, "This all happened because of you. We're going to share the success of the organization with you."[17]

Now Levine is off to a new challenge. In January 2008, the newly-elected governor of Louisiana, Piyush "Bobby" Jindal, appointed Levine secretary of his state's Department of Health and Hospitals. The health system, which is still suffering years after Hurricane Katrina, needs transformation, not repair, according to the governor.[18]

Levine leaves behind an institution capable of carrying out its mission without him. One of Broward Health's Board of Commissioners, Dan Gordon, said, "He had me and all the board members and all the staff think that we were on the verge of a world-class operation here. Two years ago, we were running a county hospital...That was a whole mind-set that he fostered. He's a forward thinker."[19] Board chairman Mike Fernandez told the press, "Alan's record of success here is impressive. Governor-elect Jindal could not have chosen a better leader. Alan leaves Broward Health a much better organization with better patient satisfaction, an improved culture of performance, financially stronger — and he leaves us believing we can be one of America's best public health systems."[20]

Smart Leaders Pursue a Mission

The framers and today's effective leaders share the understanding that the mission, as a concrete statement of current intent, provides powerful guidance for everyone to stay focused, make decisions, and take action.

The fulfillment of successive missions leads to the achievement of the vision. Successful missions are succinct and understandable by everyone: "Is there anything I can do to make you feel better?" "Clean City, Economic Development, and Customer Service," "The Preamble."

Effective leaders stay on message about the mission and create multiple ways to communicate it continuously. Managers work with employees to make sure they know specifically how their jobs relate to fulfilling the mission. Successful leaders engage every employee in getting mission-driven results and building a mission-supporting culture with meaningful incentives, not mere tokens.

Yet even if everyone wants to fulfill the mission, implementation will not happen magically. Today's leaders must take the next powerful and messy step, just as the framers did at the Convention.

Article IV

The Road Re-Traveled
The Messy Business of Generating Great Plans

Mr. Randolph [Governor of Virginia and host of the Convention] then opened the main business...He expressed his regret, that it should fall to him, rather than those, who were of longer standing in life and political experience, to open the great subject of their mission...

He then commented on the difficulty of the crisis, and the necessity of preventing the fulfillment of the prophecies of the American downfall.

He observed that in revising the federal system we ought to inquire 1. into the properties, which such a government ought to possess, 2. the defects of the confederation, 3. the danger of our situation & 4. the remedy.[1]

This early entry in James Madison's *Notes on the Constitutional Convention* encapsulates the elements of successful strategic planning used by leaders today.

Element One in Governor Randolph's message describes the mission for the planning session and defines what needs to be in any final plan. Contemporary executives often begin their planning sessions by defining where the organization needs to be in the near future. For the framers, Randolph focused on internal and external security and the need to unite against these threats.

Element Two was the Virginia delegation's analysis of the positives and negatives facing the country. Modern teams engage in the same analysis, often developing a detailed list of internal strengths and weaknesses and external opportunities and threats — a SWOT analysis.

In Element Three, Randolph elaborated on "the danger of our situation." Like modern leaders, he had performed a thorough risk analysis. The Convention delegates agreed on the dangers they faced, including the possibility of being reabsorbed into Britain or being divided up among Britain, France, and Spain. Strategic leaders do not flinch from examining the seriousness of the situation an organization faces. They know these risks must be addressed in the final plan.

Governor Randolph presented the so-called Virginia Plan, drafted by James Madison, as Element Four, the skeleton of the new Constitution, and the focal point for discussions. Successful leaders usually have a draft ready for their planning sessions, not to restrict ideas, but to stimulate people to think ahead of time and add structure to the session. At the Convention, a few other delegates had prepared sketches of a new constitution, but theirs gained little traction because they were less detailed, illustrating the importance of robust preparation for the planning session.

Randolph threw down the gauntlet when he presented the Virginia Plan. He jump-started the Convention by telling the delegates up front their goal must be a federal system "to be paramount to the state Constitutions." The new Constitution would wipe out the monopoly on power held by the states. Modern leaders do the same when they challenge their executives to reinvent the business or shatter old ways of thinking. Shaking up the status quo is the tack taken by most of the leaders interviewed for this book.

For leadership teams, the framers' approach is paramount; setting an agenda and framework for planning, analyzing the situation thoroughly, calculating the risks, and challenging everyone to think in radically new ways. As PBS&J CEO

John Zumwalt said, successful strategic leaders "put people on a mission" which leads the organization to accomplish its goals. Like Randolph, leaders articulate a mission for the planning process and keep people focused. Madison's plan purposefully painted the new government structure in broad strokes. Contemporary leaders also aim for the emergence of a strategic plan that focuses on broad goals and objectives. The details of how each objective will be met are then expanded through the efforts of various departments and individuals.

Modern leaders could use the experiences of the framers as a roadmap for strategic planning. The distance between the summer of 1787 and today is remarkably short. The best approaches, then as now, are almost identical. The primary difference is that a modern CEO may be reluctant to lock the executive team in an airless room, far from home, for four months!

Strategy Planning Requires a Planning Strategy

While modern strategic planning follows the basic pattern familiar to the Constitutional framers, modern leaders adapt the framework to their organizations.

When Howard Putnam became CEO at Southwest Airlines, he found himself in a fluid, entrepreneurial company that valued flexibility, encouraged innovation, and avoided bureaucracy. His experience at other large airlines showed him the downside of making the planning process too rigid.

After Putnam put the new vision in place and achieved a group focus, as discussed in Article II, he turned to the budget. He started out as he had at one of the big airlines. He asked to review the budget. A department head told him, "Howard, I don't have a budget. We don't spend any money unless we have to." Putnam knew he needed a budget process between the extremes of total rigidity and nothing, so he teamed up with his CFO, Phil Guthrie, who is still his partner in various ventures.

Phil and I would look at the economics of our company, not just the industry. Remember now, we're not an airline, we're in mass transportation. Our whole philosophy was, 'We'll make the pie bigger; we'll generate new travelers, not go into a market and steal from the other guy.'

We would lay out what we thought the economics were going to be for us for the next twelve months. We came up with a revenue number of $X billion. Then we'd ask, 'What rate of return on the investment do our shareholders deserve?' Then we would choose the percentage and say, 'That first $Y million goes to the shareholders.' Then we would go over to the service side and on-time performance, and price that out. 'How many employees do you need to turn an airplane in ten minutes and load the bags, etc., ninety percent of the time?'

We would come up with a macro economic plan and a potential bottom line. I would take that to the board of directors. We still haven't gone to the cost side or even zero-based budgeting. And, we hadn't gone out and bothered our managers and said, 'Start building your manpower and equipment-needs budget.' We never bothered.

Once I had the board's overall concurrence, we'd go back out to the field and say, 'Here's the general guideline.' It was in the managers' hands to come back and say, 'I can't do it that way, and here's why.' The standards were so clear and so simple that it was pretty hard for anybody to play games with us. Compared to other airlines, we just didn't waste much time in the budget-planning cycle.

Ed Novak is a former senior vice president in the

Commercial Banking division of Bank of America. In his last nine years with the company, he was responsible for the performance measurement and client profitability systems that supported the entire Commercial Banking division. BOA also had a very different, yet quite effective, approach to planning. The Bank adopted the Hoshin Planning[2] approach to strategic planning and added the Balanced Scorecard[3] method of tracking goals.

The Hoshin Planning approach "helps orchestrate the direction of the company. In this system, each manager selects his three or four most important activities which tie into the top three priorities of the company...[with a] strong focus on the means, the process by which targets are reached."[4] *Hoshin kanri* planning originated in Japan and is variously translated as 'target and means,' 'policy planning, management or control,' 'direction,' and 'management by policy.' The purpose of Hoshin is to stay focused on a limited number of goals and manage the processes that must function flawlessly to achieve those goals.

In the Balanced Scorecard methodology, goals and measurements are distributed among four distinct areas: customers, financials, employee learning and growth, and internal business processes. Everything is driven by the vision and the strategies that support it. Each goal has concrete objectives, measures, targets, and initiatives to achieve the targets. The allied approaches of Hoshin and Balanced Scorecard concentrate the company's efforts on a limited number of areas and yet expand goal setting beyond financials.

Novak's group was assigned to build the Scorecards for other groups and support them technologically. He describes his process.

> We're in the middle of the organization, so some of our marching orders come down from above. In addition to those, we welcome input from every direction, like a wagon wheel reaching out to all our stakeholders. We talk

about strategies and what's important from everyone's perspective. We do a free-wheeling brainstorming session and keep it in what we called a judgment-free zone.

Novak and his team's challenge was to take all the input and somehow shape it into a coherent plan. The team's process is similar to the various committees set up at the Constitutional Convention to wrangle the diverse decisions, ideas, arguments, and motions into an organized, prioritized plan. Just as the framers had to integrate the interests of large states and small, North and South, agriculture and trade, Novak's team was charged with putting a Scorecard together to reflect and focus the interests of everyone from the bank branch teller to the president. As Novak reports,

> Hoshin Planning is the glue that holds all this together. We align with the corporate vision, 'to be the world's most admired company.' Then we align with our own mission, 'to create a world-class commercial bank offering unparalleled resources, product and industry expertise, and grow each of our businesses and delight our clients each and every time.' Then we set our goals using the Balanced Scorecard.

Steve Hickman, like Novak, is a lifelong banker and has worked in the commercial and retail sides of the industry. Hickman founded Florida Shores Bank in 2006 to serve the large small-business community in Pompano Beach, Florida. Each new branch will base its service on the unique demographics of its community.

Hickman learned his strategic planning craft early in his career when he built a large bank's small-business program in the early 1990s.

> We had thirty-one individual banks underneath that holding company umbrella. I had to convince all thirty-

one of those banks to implement the same strategic program for dealing with a small business because each bank was independently operated. It was a collaborative, exhaustive approach to get all thirty-one banks to march in the same direction. What makes me most proud about it is, virtually every major bank in the country has adopted that strategic vision and view of how we handled small business.

When Hickman founded Florida Shores Bank, he had to decide which of two bank start-up approaches he would use. "One strategy is to start with an exit strategy and make your shareholders wealthy within a few years. The second strategy is one of longevity, and building for the long term, and creating a legacy. I chose the latter and found shareholders who would fit this approach." As Hickman sets his strategic plan in motion each year, it is aligned with this overarching legacy approach.

In building his team, he looks for people who share his passion for service to the customers. "It's all about the customer experience. When they leave, they'll remember that experience. Then we'll measure the success of that experience in how well we perform against our peers," he said. Hickman has every employee focused on building relationships, not transactions. "I had my strategy first, and then hired my team to fit that strategy. I hired people with different strengths. I don't want clones."

Starting a bank requires meeting extensive regulatory hurdles. Initially, Hickman took on the role of primary strategic planner to steer his new company through a tough economic period and meet regulatory requirements. As the bank becomes more established, he brings more and more of the team into the planning. He started by breaking down the barriers that exist in a typical bank's staff, primarily through modeling the behavior he wants and creating a culture that is respectful and gets ideas from everyone. He created a forum where *all* employees can contribute ideas. He pulls in everyone's views and captures their knowledge as he builds his SWOT analysis. It is a foundation for finding solutions that will make up the bank's plans.

Messiness: The Hallmark of Great Planning

No matter how good the content of any formal planning methodology or reference text, it cannot capture the dynamic nature of planning itself. In fact, great planning sessions are often downright messy. In Article VII, you'll read about the often raucous debates that flared as the Convention wore on and tempers wore thin. The framers complained endlessly about the conditions they faced. As state currencies collapsed and inflation soared, merchants in Philadelphia refused to take the paper money, issued by state legislatures, the delegates tried to use. They only accepted a bewildering array of foreign coins because they had value, unlike the states' often worthless currency.

Richard Spaight, a delegate from North Carolina, wrote throughout the summer asking for money. "I fear that much time will be expended in this business, much more than I expected...and of course another supply of cash must take place to enable us to stay here."[5] This plea came at the end of May, and in July he appealed again, reminding the state that his salary was two months overdue. "My cash is already expended. Judge then my situation should I receive no further supplies."[6] By September he wrote plaintively, "My situation here is extremely distressing...[I] shall be here till tomorrow week, when I hope to get away provided I can get money to pay off my Accounts here and bear my expenses home, which I have no other means of doing than by borrowing." Even that would require a friend signing a note and the state sending money to repay it quickly.[7] New Jersey delegate William Paterson wrote to his wife, "I shall be in want of some hard money in order to clear me of this town...it is no end for me to draw upon the Jersey treasury, as it contains nothing but paper money, which few people will take."[8]

The delegates complained even more vociferously about the amount of time the debates were taking. Delegates sometimes took to their feet for hours or continued on into the next day. Today's team members may start fidgeting when someone blathers on for ten or fifteen minutes. In fact, more and more people start thumbing through electronic messages if someone starts to bore them. Men of the eighteenth century were used to sitting through long speeches and debates, yet some of the real windbags were too much even for them. In the long, contentious debates around representation in the new Congress,

> [Maryland delegate] Luther Martin chose this most inopportune time, and in a spell of hot weather, too, to deliver a lengthy harangue. For more than three hours he continued and, having exhausted his own strength, to say nothing of the patience of his audience, he announced to the dismay of all that he would resume his discourse the next day...[Later Connecticut delegate Oliver] Ellsworth scathingly wrote to Martin: "You opened against them in a speech which held during two days, and which might have continued two months, but for those marks of fatigue and disgust you saw strongly expressed on whichever side of the house you turned your mortified eyes"...[Madison] complained of the difficulty of following what Martin said, for he spoke "with much diffuseness and considerable vehemence."[9]

If Men were Angels, No Government would be Necessary
– James Madison

Why did the Convention drag on for so long? What can modern leaders learn from the experience? In part, the length can be attributed to the seriousness of their task, the need to be thorough, and their desire to make the new Constitution as correct as possible. Other contributors to the length were so many different points of view and interests, the less frenetic pace of the framers' lives, and the lack of incessant, instant communication. As important as all of these causes were, the delegates set up several crucial rules for themselves, which assured lengthy debate.

They were all versed in parliamentary procedure and generally accepted rules of debate and meeting decorum. We have a stereotyped view of them – dressed in their finery, engaging in edifying and enlightening discussions, always genteel and polite, and using elaborate, courteous language. It's an illusion. Although it's true their eighteenth-century language was more elaborate and they were seldom as blunt and profane in public as we are, they had honed the put-down into high art and their sarcasm to a lethal knife edge.

That's why one of the first tasks they took on when they assembled in Philadelphia was the creation of a set of rules to govern their meetings. The list is interesting, because it points out just what sort of bad behavior they expected.

> Every member, rising to speak, shall address the President; and whilst he shall be speaking, none shall pass between them, or hold discourse with another, or read a book, pamphlet or paper, printed or manuscript...
>
> A member shall not speak oftener than twice...upon the same questions...before every other who had been silent, shall have been heard, if he choose to speak upon a subject...
>
> A member may be called to order by any other member, as well as by the President; and may be allowed to explain his conduct or expressions supposed to be reprehensible...[10]

They adopted these additional rules that ensured protracted discussions.

> That no copy be taken of any entry on the journal during the sitting of the House without leave of the House.
> That members only be permitted to inspect the journal.
>
> That nothing spoken in the House be printed, or otherwise published or communicated without leave.
> That a motion to reconsider a matter which had been determined by a majority, may be made...[11]

By maintaining absolute secrecy and allowing issues to be reconsidered, they ensured creative ideas could be floated without ridicule or later political or other repercussions. Although the press and public speculated wildly (and wrongly) on what was happening in the Pennsylvania Statehouse that summer, there were no leaks, no anonymous sources, and no later character assassinations based on some idea that went nowhere. Although there were a few slips and planted innuendos over the years, the delegates abided by their rules for the most part and had open, honest, and far-ranging discussions.

They did chafe under the restrictions, as was evident when a delegate who had left the Convention wrote to another late in August:

> [What's going on at the Convention?] When will they rise? Will they agree upon a System energetick and effectual, or will they break up without doing any Thing to the Purpose? Full of Disputation and noisy as the Wind, it is said, that you are afraid of the very Windows, and have a Man planted under them to prevent the Secrets and Doings from flying out...I wish you much Speed, and that you may be full of good Works...for I dread going down again to Philada.—

My Compliments to all your Fellow-Labourers under the Same Roof.[12]

Coming to Consensus

The debate over how representation in the new government would be organized was one of the thorniest issues the delegates tackled. The Virginia Plan called for two Houses, with representation in each based more or less on population. This stood in stark contrast to the Confederation Congress, which allowed only one vote per state. The larger states, stymied time and time again by the smaller states under the Confederation, favored the new system. The small states resisted proportional representation, fearing their voice would be lost and they would be overwhelmed and swallowed by the larger states.

The debate raged. Many proposals were put forth, committees formed, and old ideas were thrown out to the group again. A committee would offer a compromise, and the factions would attack it. No one really wanted to budge. Each interest group had its position to protect. It was a complex and intricate dance of North vs. South, East vs. West, and nationalists vs. state's rights proponents. As the debates wore on, some delegates left the Convention, never to return. At one point, someone suggested that Rhode Island, which had refused to participate, be contacted to send delegates, but that was seen as a ploy to boost the fortunes of the small-state faction.

If any issue threatened to break up the Convention, it was how representation would be established. As votes continued, it became clear that the lower House would represent population. Back they went to committee for more refinement.

Modern teams often become frustrated when some decision is reopened. They grumble about paralysis by analysis. But the very fact that someone has a new view on a hot topic is significant. The process of coming to consensus is messy, repetitive, and even annoying, but ensures that the final decision is more fully vetted.

When the convention finally got at the question of proportional representation, nearly three weeks were spent in reaching a conclusion. More than once any satisfactory solution of the difficulty seemed impossible, and the convention was on the point of breaking up. Gouverneur Morris afterwards said that 'the fate of America was suspended by a hair.' Feeling ran high at the very outset, and Franklin interposed with a motion that 'prayers imploring the assistance of Heaven...be held in this Assembly every morning'...[A]pprehension was expressed lest such a step at this late day might lead the public to suspect that there were dissensions in the convention. There is also a tradition that Hamilton opposed the motion on the ground that the convention was not in need of 'foreign aid.' The real cause...[was] 'the convention had no funds.'[13]

Although Franklin's suggestion on prayer was ignored, his pleas for compromise were not. Several people, including Roger Sherman, delegate from Connecticut, had proposed a compromise solution. And so the summer dragged on. They hammered away at bits and pieces of the recommendations of the committees and modified them beyond recognition. Finally, a committee came back with something the delegates could agree on, because neither small nor large states could get their way completely. On July 16, the Convention passed the "great compromise."

This is the great compromise of the convention and of the constitution. None other is to be placed quite in comparison with it...The important feature of the compromise was that in the upper house of the legislature each state should have an equal vote. The principle of proportional representation in the lower house was not a part of the compromise, although the details for carrying out that principle were involved...

With proportional popular representation established for one house, equal state representation for the other was inevitable, both from the ideas of representation that were current at the time and from the division of opinions in the convention.[14]

Despite its meandering digression, occasional hot-tempered exchanges, and retracing the same trail, the messy process eventually brought a consensus agreement. The final plan was one that all but three of the remaining delegates could agree to, sign, and pass to the people for ratification. For modern teams, the challenge is still to allow discussions to lurch toward consensus. Executive team members are often restive after even a short discussion, and want to move things along more quickly. A strong leader must slow down the process so the team walks toward consensus, even with some diversions and loops, rather than runs toward a hasty, and wrong, so-called "solution."

Great Planning Requires Inclusiveness

Walking toward consensus has become a hallmark of Clarence Otis' tenure as CEO of Darden Restaurants. He began his career in investment banking before making the move to General Mills. When the company spun off its Darden Restaurants division, he became treasurer of the casual dining chain, working with CEO Joe Lee. For Otis, Lee was "an inclusive leader who could mobilize the whole officer group." Under Lee's mentorship, Otis took on a number of challenging assignments, including CFO. When Lee retired, Otis became chairman and CEO and brought Lee's inclusive leadership style into his own work.

We start with our vision, and then how we are going to organize our planning so that we communicate that vision. But we also have to understand from the people closest to the action, what's going on in our restaurants and with our customers. Then we broaden it out to leaders from our two biggest operating companies, Red Lobster and Olive Garden.

Ultimately, we're talking about two time horizons. What is it we want to do longer term, and which direction do we want to go in? In the next twelve months, what are the strategic initiatives we need to be working on to make the five-year plan happen? What do we need to do to run the business effectively for the next twelve months and reach our short-term objectives?

Otis cascades the planning process down through each of the operating companies so they can focus on the next twelve months, guided by the strategic initiatives. He and his teams spend five months each year actively engaged in this planning cycle. They launch each annual plan with massive communication that continues in several media throughout the year. Eventually, each restaurant manager is brought into the process and works with staff to make the plans a reality in the individual restaurants. The goal is to create the customer experience that defines the business. Otis created a system focused on building robust processes that help over one hundred fifty thousand employees in over fifteen hundred restaurants stay focused on the overall strategy. He has been able to do this despite the near-complete employee turnover at the hourly level that is standard in the restaurant industry. Otis' practice of inclusiveness is the secret to making the planning system effective.

I develop an environment up front where people are as candid as possible. I encourage that. We provide a lot of factual information from our extensive research so people won't be guided by opinion. We want them to say, 'This is my sense of what those facts might mean.' Then their judgment comes into play – and it is often intuitive, and that drives creativity. We try to teach everyone to respect that intuition and creativity informed by experience. I encourage people to listen and respect their experience.

Being inclusive was not a strong suit for the framers. Their republican ideals rested more on assuring everyone representation, not including everyone directly in decision-making. As Jefferson's more *democratic* ideas took hold and began to blossom in the nineteenth century, the notion of inclusiveness expanded. Yet, it would take wars, mass immigration and westward migration, industrialization, and movements for social and political change over the nineteenth and twentieth centuries to see the modern notion of inclusiveness emerge. Even with the limited notion of inclusiveness in the last decades of the eighteenth century, the composition of the representatives in the state conventions set up to ratify the new Constitution was far more representative and inclusive than it had been up to that point in most states. In fact, the lack of inclusiveness in the Constitutional Convention resulted in some of their most far-reaching bad decisions, to be discussed in Article V.

Greg Swienton, CEO of Ryder System, is a modern executive who emphasizes inclusiveness in the company's planning process. First, he works with his senior team to set the overall strategic direction. That executive team depends on another dedicated team to come up with all the background information on industries, markets, competitiveness, and customers' needs. Eventually, every level of the corporation, from the board of directors to the managers in every division, is involved, looking at market needs and what each division can provide.

It's probably not that different from the framers getting together and thinking about how they would write a Constitution. It's our blueprint. You look at all the possibilities, and at the things you can be doing and what you're already doing. It's an opportunity to get together and think things through and have everybody express themselves. We want everybody to express opinions, pro and con, so when we leave, we have a general direction.

Evan Rees brought the inclusiveness approach with him when he became President of the South Florida region, operating a start-up bank for CNL Finance. CNL is one of the largest privately-held commercial real estate investment companies in the U.S. Rees, who has a degree in agriculture, likes to use Stephen Covey's "law of the harvest" metaphor. As Rees paraphrases Covey, "You have to prepare the soil you want to plant. There is a certain process you have to continually go through in order to reap the rewards…and it's a long-term process."

One of the first things Rees did was work with his team to create a strategic plan and then delegate the details to his branch managers. The branch plans are more tactical, as suits a start-up operation. Rees focused on "moving the big rocks first and getting the important people in place first, and then the important processes, so we could transact business on a fairly smooth basis. Then I can focus on doing what I do best, recruiting and marketing." He found the key challenge was keeping people focused. That focus emerged as they worked on their own plans.

At MinuteClinic, former CEO Michael Howe found he was in a similar inclusive situation. His planning involvement at companies from Arby's to PepsiCo had employed a very formal process.

You never really thought about planning much outside the annual structure. Here, it's totally different. Part of that is because it's health care and part is the ambiguity.

Here, we have to unleash the creativity. We all have whiteboards in our offices and we spend most of our time mapping out our ideas on them. It's interesting. We start doodling on the board by ourselves, and other people wander in and join us.

For example, we were talking about how we open new clinics. I just started putting some big buckets on the whiteboard, and then we started asking ourselves, 'What does it take? What do we have to do?' Then the incubation of ideas starts. You'll walk around the office and see everybody's got different ideas they're working on. That's really planning. The planning process here is almost daily, where before it was annual. We don't know what the rules are. No one's gone before us. So we keep taking feedback through the day from different sources and just keep adding to the experience, adding ideas. We draw, we erase, we draw. The neat thing about it is it's a living process.

Eventually, for Howe and his team, this messy process proceeds to a conclusion, just as the Constitutional Convention did. The team pulls enough ideas together to develop the budget and formalize a plan. But the process remains fluid as they implement to adjust to the evolving culture they are trying to create. "The execution becomes more disciplined, but the planning tends to be very open-ended," he said. In some respects, Howe's approach is like that of the framers as they transitioned into the new government and had to turn their ideas into actions. As we might say today, they had to make it up as they went along.

Messiness Rules

Many of the leaders interviewed had some experience with planning in large corporations that had become too bureaucratic and stifled the creative energy necessary for success. Although the *organizational* details varied from company to company, all the leaders had incorporated ways to involve people at every level in the planning process. They built on as much factual knowledge and experience as they could muster, and encouraged the messy process of creativity to ensure vital, robust plans for both the long and short term. They got people *involved* in planning. That made it easier for them to take responsibility and exercise their authority wisely.

These contemporary leaders instinctively followed the pattern of the framers. They escaped the constricting confines of ossified planning methodologies, generated as many ideas from as many points of view as possible, and allowed the discussion to roam over a wide territory. Eventually, they brought the team to consensus, a place where they all agreed to implement a common solution that reflected their diverse views.

But this messy and creative process is not always foolproof, as the framers and today's leaders discovered. Individuals and teams can make very bad decisions. How do they fall into the trap? Can these traps be avoided? How do leaders handle mistakes, bad decisions, and general wrong-headedness?

Article V

"Mistakes Were Made"
The Gift that Keeps on Giving

The Constitution of the United States

Article. I
Section 2.

...Representatives and direct Taxes shall be apportioned among the several States...[and] shall be determined by adding to the whole Number of free Persons...three fifths of all other Persons

Section 9

...Importation of such Persons...shall not be prohibited by the Congress prior to the Year one thousand eight hundred and eight...

We've all seen CEOs doing the "perp walk" on the eleven o'clock news, expensive suit jackets crumpled and stretched over their heads, a phalanx of lawyers guiding with one hand and stiff-arming reporters out of the way with the other, a grim, stunned spouse following. We watch the former executives of Enron, WorldCom, Tyco, and Adelphia with disgust while the cynical tar all corporate leaders with the same brush.

These business scandals confirmed many people's beliefs about corporate greed and egos run amok. In his latest book, Lee Iacocca asked, "Will we ever trust corporate America again?...A lot of corporate executives must have been paying close attention in 1987 when the actor Michael Douglas uttered those famous words in the movie *Wall Street*: 'Greed is good.' They took heart...The most prevalent motto of corporate America seems to be greed. You ask someone to name a top business leader and they think of the guy they just saw being led away in handcuffs."[1] Iacocca points out that the employees not only lose their jobs, but also their savings and pensions. Stockholders lose their investments. Often the culprits, who are wearing golden handcuffs as well as steel ones, keep their McMansions and mega-millions while they're in the pokey.

The catch phrase, "mistakes were made," rolls readily off the tongue today in press conferences. This awkward and meaningless phrase is designed for the guilty to escape personal responsibility. True leaders fess up and take responsibility.

Most corporate leaders are *not* criminals. Yet they can make colossal blunders, including ones that amuse us. New Coke and the Ford Edsel were introduced with great fanfare and bombed immediately. Everyone laughed and played Monday-morning quarterback.

The challenge for leaders is to understand *how* these mistakes come about and what they should *do* when a mistake is discovered. Great leaders learn from their mistakes and apply the lessons to new situations.

The leaders discussed in this book were forthcoming about their mistakes, but as Ryder System CEO Greg Swienton remarked, "I haven't had any so bad that it's killed my career. I probably wouldn't have this job." As George Washington paraphrased Shakespeare, *to err is natural, to rectify error is glory.*[2]

The Anatomy of a Bad Decision

In constructing the Constitution, the framers *did* make some big mistakes. Their initial voting system in the Electoral College broke down very quickly and had to be amended.[3]

The delegates failed to add a Bill of Rights, which threatened to derail ratification in several states. The first Congress quickly passed the first ten amendments to the Constitution, rectifying the mistake. It took more than one hundred years to enfranchise women and almost two hundred years to ensure the rights of black voters and citizens. But the most glaring error of the framers was enshrining slavery in the Constitution.

The word *slavery* never appears; the delegates to the Convention assuaged their consciences by never using the word in the document. Instead, they substituted code words that everyone understood, such as "persons held in Service or Labour" or "other persons." Some people argue that without the compromise on slavery, no agreement would have been possible. Others say the framers had various remedies they could have chosen that would have ended slavery.

Was slavery one of the necessary compromises to get agreement on a new Constitution? Was it like the so-called Great Compromise on representation that accommodated the states' power concerns? Or, was the compromise on slavery a mistake that could have been avoided? Some of the framers and their contemporaries believed it was a devastating error. Even Thomas Jefferson, a slave owner, predicted the issue would eventually destroy the Union. Unfortunately, he was almost proven correct.

How Do Good Leaders Make Bad Decisions?

How do leaders, whether the framers or contemporary executives, make bad decisions? The framers and today's leaders can literally become "framed." That word shouldn't be confused with bad guys in a gangster movie hollering, "I wuz framed!" as they're hauled off to jail. People are "framed" in a more significant and sometimes mystifying psychological way. Think of this sort of frame as a box that limits our view of possibilities and alternatives. Framing doesn't let you off the hook. It simply describes a common situation that strategic leaders learn to acknowledge and overcome.

Luda Kopeikina, CEO of Noventra, studied the framing phenomenon among executives who were in the throes of decision-making and documented it in her book, *The Right Decision Every Time*.[4]

> By its nature, any decision perspective is limiting. It puts a decision into a frame, highlighting certain elements and hiding the rest. A wrong decision perspective presents a major difficulty in arriving at a clear choice...we rarely spontaneously question the formulation of a problem or the underlying personal or business assumptions behind our current perspective. We rarely reframe instinctively...
>
> Frames come from the way the problem is presented to you...tinted with other parties' opinions, media expectations, and other environmental factors...[and] from unrecognized personal and business assumptions, attitudes and habits.

Consider the following bad decisions by several contemporary leaders, whose identifying information, gender, and names have been disguised.[5] In retrospect, they identified the frames which blinded them to other actions. Their frames are common ones occurring every day in organizations.

* * * * * * * * *

Mark G was "very big on loyalty and honor." He hired an executive, who secretly kept his former job. When this executive announced he was going back to the old job, Mark admits, "I went over into the red zone." He called the president of the company the man was returning to and reported the duplicity. The president fired the man, who then sued Mark and his company. "It was one of the worst decisions I ever made and I learned from it. Always take the high road, even when the other person is one hundred percent wrong."

* * * * * * * * *

Sam L's company had an opportunity to make a large investment in another company. Although the numbers looked good, "there was something unsettling about it." The investment was a disaster and Sam's company couldn't recoup all the money. "Listen to your gut and experience. Take them into consideration along with the 'facts' to make a more holistic, better decision."

* * * * * * * * *

Charles J's company faced major challenges during an economic downturn and, assuming the decline in results was completely due to economic factors, he didn't look further. "It was a trap. A very reasonable assumption just wasn't true. The real cause was poor internal performance. I learned, no matter what seems obvious, dig in deeper. Otherwise, you put pressure on people to fix it, and it's hard on everyone."

* * * * * * * * *

Nancy B installed a person in an executive position who was "more of a structure and control type of person. Her position has a lot of impact on the people. She tends to dampen the empowerment that we stand for. All it takes is something bad to happen and then she swings too far to the control side. I should have made the hard decision, not put her in the wrong position, and stood up to the inevitable criticism."

* * * * * * * * *

Martin O figured out too late he needed to make changes to his board of directors. "I realized we needed people who could add value, not just agree with us. Now it's hard to take any action."

* * * * * * * * *

Don J "made some doozies" when he reacted rather than reflected. "In the midst of heated negotiations, I got an e-mail suggesting some drastic action about those who differed with us. I hit 'reply all' and said, 'I couldn't agree with you more and here are the culprits.' That e-mail ended up in the newspaper!" Don's boss had him call the people immediately and apologize. "It was hard to be humble and admit my mistake, but most of the people accepted it. You make a mistake, you admit it, and then you work to correct it."

* * * * * * * * *

Bill T learned the same lesson when he moved to save money through eliminating a department and dividing its work among others. "I had a major misunderstanding with one of the department heads. I could have jammed it down everyone's throat, but I realized I made a mistake. I got applause for changing my mind and doing what turned out to be the right thing. If you made a mistake, admit it, get out quick, and fix it."

* * * * * * * * *

Tom K went to a new company as an executive, but with a big chip on his shoulder. "I walked in saying, 'I am terrific!' I put results before relationships. We created phenomenal results, but I killed every relationship." He realized he had alienated the whole team. "I destroyed any chance of support and connection with these people. I had no option, I had to leave. I said, 'never again.' It prompted me to think more about the environment I wanted to create and valuing the relationships and connections I needed to be effective."

* * * * * * * *

Mary L was in a new position and took over part of the work of her strongest performer. "I lied and said it was so I could learn the business. That was a mask. What I really wanted was some work I enjoyed. The person quit. Two weeks later he showed up at headquarters, working for someone else. I figured out I was the liability. I lost a valuable employee instead of leveraging his skill."

* * * * * * * *

In each case, these leaders framed the problem from the wrong perspective and went down the wrong path. Their common 'mis-frames' were:

- Making decisions in negative emotional states, such as anger or fear;
- Mismatching talent and the job;
- Being blinded by strictly budgetary savings;
- Failing to listen to one's gut and experience;
- Failing to question *all* assumptions;
- Failing to analyze all one's needs;
- Failing to understand the need for relationship building;
- Failing to value team member expertise.

When these leaders recognized their framing mistakes, they could move beyond the frame, gain a new perspective, and make better future decisions. The problem is, we cannot always recognize these frames when we're inside them. Kopeikina's methodology begins with the caveat, "Always assume that you are framed."

> Before resolving a difficult issue...make it a practice to identify alternative frames and shift your perspective – ensuring that you are making the decision from the right perspective. You often reach clarity by shifting your view of the problem until you find the one that clicks...The ability to reframe is a skill – the more you do it, the better you will be at it.[6]

What Were the Framers' 'Frames?'

Return to the framers and the Convention, not to second guess them, but to look at their actual situation. How did their frames prevent them from finding alternative solutions that were known to them at the time? George Washington's advice will guide the discussion, *"We ought not to look back unless it is to derive useful lessons from past errors, and for the purpose of profiting by dear-bought experience."*[7]

The slavery debate was complex, not a simple standoff between Northerners who did not own slaves and Southerners who did. Another oversimplification is that Southerners were all racists by today's standards and did not believe slavery was wrong. The actual situation is not so clear-cut.

In 1787, slavery existed in most of the thirteen states. For example, New York had a slave population of about twenty thousand at the time. The big difference was the greater economic dependence on slavery in the South. After the Convention and the establishment of the new federal government, many northern states began abolishing the practice. Some individual delegates also freed their slaves.

While the Convention was meeting in Philadelphia, the Confederation Congress was meeting in New York City. Congress passed the Northwest Ordinance in mid-July, which banned slavery in the Northwest Territory, the land north of the Ohio River. The delegates at the Constitutional Convention knew the details immediately. The ordinance set the context for both the decisions in the Convention and in the state ratifying conventions.[8]

> In Pennsylvania, [James] Wilson assured [state] ratification delegates that the new Congress would honor this aspect of the Northwest Ordinance. He began by predicting that in 1808 [when the Constitution barred further import of slaves] Congress would likely end the 'reproachful' transatlantic slave trade and thereby lay 'the foundation for banishing slavery out of this country' via a 'gradual change'...No prominent Southern Federalist during the ratification process contradicted Wilson's early public statements...

> When the First Congress convened, it quickly redeemed Wilson's pledge, enacting a statute designed to give 'full effect' to the principles of the Northwest Ordinance... in August 1789 as the new nation's eighth public law... In 1820, as part of the Missouri Compromise, a later Congress excluded slavery from the Louisiana Purchase territory north of the latitude line 36° 30'. Before adding his signature to this act, [the President] Virginian James Monroe polled his cabinet, which included the staunch South Carolinian slavocrat John C. Calhoun and several other leading slave-state politicians. The group unanimously affirmed the...rule's constitutionality [establishing so called 'free-soil' states and territories that prohibited slavery.]

> Even this positive part of the compromise was spliced with

the baser side of human nature. Behind the scenes, complicated deal-making took place in both the Confederation Congress and the Constitutional Convention. The complex negotiations involved allying Northern and Southern land speculators, bullying by a powerful congressman, alleged manipulating by Alexander Hamilton, making intricate deals on trade and navigation acts, and enshrining, in both the Northwest Ordinance and the Constitution, the ability of slave owners to pursue and re-enslave those who escaped to freedom.

Many historians see the subtle evidence of backroom deals. For example, on July 11, Gouverneur Morris made a strong anti-Southern speech. On the following morning, he opened the session with a new proposal linking representation and taxation formulas in a manner "which bridged the North-South conflict. This swift shift of position suggests that something had been worked out overnight."[9]

Even without the speculation on what was happening behind the scenes (and there is scant hard evidence, because the players did not record their machinations in their voluminous diaries and letters), the framers' public speeches record a complex set of views and a willingness to do what was necessary to form a union and government that would work. Their compromises were complicated, and their perception frames complex.

Many of the Virginia elite represented at the Convention were keen on ending the *importation* of slaves because they had more slaves than they needed. They wanted to create an incentive for states in the Deep South to purchase slaves from them. Slave owners such as Washington, Jefferson, and Madison, as well as many non-slave owners, were typical of people throughout the country who believed slavery would slowly disappear. There are further complexities in the debates. Madison found slavery personally abhorrent, but never spoke out against it in the Convention. On the other hand, George Mason, who owned about two hundred slaves, spoke out against it vehemently.

Complicating the debates about slavery were issues of commerce and navigation, population densities, the demographics and economies of the future states to be carved out of the western territories, how representation would be structured to provide balance between North and South, regional animosities between New England and the Deep South, whether the government should conduct a periodic census for reapportionment, whether population or wealth should be the basis for taxation and/or representation, whether exports should be taxed, and a variety of other seemingly unrelated issues that were all directly tied to slavery.

Like the framers, contemporary leaders do not step into their major decisions lightly. Crucial decisions about the direction of the organization are often a complicated dance of economics, markets, history, personal biases, legal considerations, politics, and other competing and conflicting factors.

The Framers' 'Frames' Revealed[10]

Going into the Convention, delegates thought the biggest splits would be between the large and small states. After a compromise was reached on representation, almost every other major difference hinged on slavery.

For example, James McHenry, writing for the Maryland delegation as it caucused, expressed the South's position seemingly on the federal government controlling navigation and trade.

> '[T]he dearest interests of trade' would be under the control of four large states. What then would become of the Southern export trade?... 'We almost shuddered... at the fate of the commerce of Maryland, should we be unable to make a change in this extraordinary power [to regulate commerce and navigation]...'[O]ur deputation ought never to assent to this.'[11]

These words were a veiled threat to vote against any agreement that threatened the slave trade or taxed export of slaves, cotton, indigo, rice, tobacco, and foodstuffs from the agricultural South.

Reading those charged words allows us to feel the political heat that rose with the thermometer in Philadelphia, to sense the passion and sarcasm that flowed. Anger bubbled, as some representatives dug in and refused to compromise. They clearly understood that their own self-interest asserted itself in every decision, yet they had trouble escaping their perception frames — even when they recognized them. And, like some of the modern leaders we interviewed, they were framed by their emotions.

As the latest draft of the Constitution was brought up for discussion on August 8, the debate quickly boiled. This heated exchange was not the first time delegates talked about slavery but it illustrates how the issue framed so many other issues. The row began as they discussed the following proposed passage on taxation:[12]

> The proportions of direct taxation shall be regulated by the whole number of white and other free citizens and inhabitants of every age, sex and condition, including those bound to servitude for a term of years [indentured servants,] and three fifths of all other persons [slaves] not comprehended in the foregoing description...

In other words, taxation and representation in the House of Representatives would be based on the number of free citizens plus three-fifths of the enslaved population. The Southern delegates believed this would give them parity with the more densely populated North. In addition, the Southerners were determined to prevent taxation on their exports of agricultural products and limit import taxes on new slaves. The North wanted to see the national government regulate all navigation and import and export trade to eliminate the interstate disputes about river use, fishing rights, and boundary lines.

The delegates engaged in bare-knuckled debate, with venomous attacks and eviscerating sarcasm. In the following dramatization,[13] spot the framers' "frames" that prevented them from finding better solutions. At the same time, think about your own team and its arguments and disagreements over major issues. Do you see the same sort of frames at work?

* * * * * * * * *

Pennsylvania State House, July - August 1787[14]

Men sit, two to a green baize-covered table, facing the dais where George Washington, erect in his chair, presides over the debate. The "three-fifths" rule for taxation has just passed, allowing each slave to be counted as three-fifths of a person to calculate state tax levies. The unmerciful sun seeps through the closed shutters. The delegates are tired and grumpy after months of debate. They now take up apportioning the legislative representation. The suggestion is to invoke the three-fifths rule again.

Rufus King, representing Massachusetts, leaps to his feet. "The admission of slaves into the rule of Representation is a most grating circumstance to my mind, and I believe it will be to a great part of the people of America." He lambastes the assembly for codifying a system where non-slave states will be forced to defend slave states against slave rebellion, presenting the odious consequence of making the government defend slave masters. "There is so much inequality and unreasonableness in all this...Either slaves should not be used to determine representation, or exports should be taxable."[15]

Roger Sherman, a delegate from Connecticut, has been horse-trading behind the scenes with the South Carolina delegation. Their alliance lasts for most of the convention, resulting in many of the compromises on slavery the convention makes.[16]

Don't be misled by his voice of reason and compromise. It is political weaseling and a failure to lead based on his backroom deal. "I regard the slave trade as iniquitous. But using slave numbers to determine representation has been settled after much difficulty and deliberation. I won't oppose it."

Gouverneur Morris, a Pennsylvania delegate, moves to the front of the stuffy, crowded room, his peg leg beating a staccato rhythm, his usual conviviality vanished. He casts a withering eye on the Southern delegates and speaks these damning and prophetic words. "I move that the word 'free' be inserted before the word inhabitants...I never will concur in upholding domestic slavery. It is a nefarious institution. It is the curse of heaven on the states where it prevails.

"Upon what principle is it that the slaves shall be computed in the representation? Are they men? Then make them Citizens and let them vote. Are they property? Why, then, is no other property included?

"Using slaves in the representation formula comes to this: an inhabitant of South Carolina, who goes to the Coast of Africa, and in defiance of the most sacred laws of humanity tears away his fellow creatures from their families and damns them to the most cruel bondages, shall have more votes in a Government instituted for protection of the rights of mankind, than the Citizen of Pennsylvania, who views this nefarious practice with a laudable horror... I would sooner submit myself to a tax for paying for all the Negroes in the United States [to be free], than saddle posterity with such a Constitution."

Sherman again tries disingenuously to smooth over the obvious chasm that has opened. "I don't think using the Negroes in the ratio of representation should raise so many objections. After all, it is the freemen of the Southern states who are to be represented according to the taxes paid by them."

Charles Pinckney from South Carolina injects another diversion. "I consider the fisheries and the Western frontier as more burdensome to the U.S. than the slaves." This seemingly bizarre statement reflects the South's fear that expansion westward will dilute their economic power through trade along the Mississippi. The South also resents the New England fisheries that complicate trade relations with Britain and France. When the question is called, only New Jersey votes to insert *free* inhabitants in the motion.

* * * * * * * * *

Modern executives, like the Convention delegates, can become more entrenched in their positions as the rhetoric heats up, and emotions become more inflamed. Corporate politics are seldom left outside the planning session and, like the Constitutional framers, people may use obfuscation, diversions, and hidden deals to further their own interests over those of the organization. In the midst of these overheated frames, consideration of vision, mission, and the needs and goals of the corporation evaporate. It is not uncommon, however, for people to couch ideas in the context of loftier aims. Perceptive leaders must sort out the sincere from the opportunistic and see through not only their own frames, but also those of others.

* * * * * * * * *

Pennsylvania State House, August 21 and 22, 1787[17]

The notorious curmudgeon, Luther Martin of Maryland, rises and reiterates earlier arguments about the cost of defending slave owners against rebellion. He suggests stopping the importation of slaves because the three-fifths rule encourages importing even more slaves. "Slaves weaken one part of the Union, the South, which the North is bound to protect. The privilege of importing slaves is therefore unreasonable. It is inconsistent with the principles of the revolution and dishonorable to the American character to have such a feature in the Constitution."

South Carolina delegate John Rutledge will not be shamed into giving up the slave trade, even when confronted by such a direct attack. "I don't worry about slave insurrections, and would readily exempt the other states from protecting the South against them. Religion and humanity have nothing to do with this question...The true question at present is whether the Southern states shall or shall not be parties to the Union."

The threat of disunion is made over and over by the representatives of the Deep South. Although everyone present knows the Southern states could not make it on their own without New England shipping their products or help defending against the Spanish on their flanks, the delegates cave.[18] They allow the frame of the necessity of creating a strong union to become their primary vulnerability to this blatant blackmail.

* * * * * * * * *

Veiled threats and passive-aggressive maneuvering are just as common in modern teams as they were with the framers, especially when other arguments are not winning the day. Like all frames, these can lead to poor decisions and big mistakes. The emotions take over, and sound decision-making and judgment decline.

Consider the cases of two different executive teams.[19] In Amalgamated Widget, two of the executives developed an intense loathing for one another. In Apex Corporation, three executives created a Bermuda Triangle where one executive was at war with the other two. At both companies, executive team meetings were more like elaborate chess matches in which the players focused almost exclusively on checkmating one another.

At Amalgamated, one of the protagonists finally backed off and the team became more functional. At Apex, when the person at war with the other two left the company, the remaining executives began functioning more normally.

In both cases, weak leaders allowed the blatant emotional framing to interfere with good decision-making.

* * * * * * * * *

Pennsylvania State House, August 21 and 22, 1787[20]

Oliver Ellsworth of Connecticut trots out a different appeasement. "Let every state import what it pleases. The morality or wisdom of slavery is a consideration belonging to the states themselves...The old Confederation did not meddle with this point, and I do not see any greater necessity for bringing it within the policy of the new one."

Pinkney jumps up to renew his threat. "South Carolina can never agree to the Constitution if it prohibits the slave trade...If we are all left alone about slavery, South Carolina may, perhaps by degrees, eliminate it on our own."

Sherman intervenes again to support his secret Southern partners. "I disapprove of the slave trade. However, since the states now possess the right to import slaves and it's important to have as few objections as possible to the proposed Constitution, I think it best to leave the matter as we find it. The abolition of slavery seems to be going on in the U.S., and the good sense of the states will probably eliminate it by degrees."

Pinkney and others repeat the implication that they may get rid of the odious slave trade on their own; a sham argument trotted out again by segregationists in the twentieth-century Civil Rights struggles. Sherman bolsters their arguments about slavery's decline. While some delegates recognized the argument as bogus, they chose to *hope* it was true, another disastrous frame.

* * * * * * * * *

Contemporary leaders often fall into the hope trap when

they announce major new initiatives in the company, but fail to create the infrastructure these changes need to survive. They hope people will change their human nature and act against their perceived best interests. Hope alone is not a strategy that works. Some of the delegates and modern leaders allow themselves to be lulled by hope.

The leaders of Apex and Amalgamated, mentioned earlier, both kept expressing hope the warring executives would see the havoc they were creating and reconcile. They hoped the next team meeting would be better, but never took effective action to make that happen. The hope frame allowed them to ignore reality and their responsibilities, and make a disastrous decision of non-intervention. Weak decision-making followed.

* * * * * * * * *

Pennsylvania State House, August 22, 1787[21]

George Mason of Virginia was a vocal critic of the slave trade, although he never freed his own slaves. He echoes the pre-Revolutionary sentiment that slavery was imposed on the colonies by the British, who would not let Virginia stop importation. Jefferson tried and failed to insert the same argument in the Declaration of Independence.

Mason points out how Virginia and Maryland have stopped importing slaves, issues a prescient warning, and obfuscates with the blame game. "Every master of slaves is born a petty tyrant. They bring the judgment of heaven on a Country... Providence punishes national sins by national calamities. I lament that some of our New England brethren have, from a lust of gain, embarked in this nefarious traffic." Mason illustrates continued blindness to his own frame, slave-owning. Modern leaders report when they dissect a bad decision, they often discover their own blind spots, their frames. By definition, they are extremely difficult to see in the midst of decision-making.

Ellsworth speaks out, sarcasm dripping, as he calls the South's bluff, but again embraces the strategy of false hope. "As I have never owned a slave, I cannot judge of the effects of slavery on character. However, if it is to be considered in a moral light, we ought to go farther and free those already in the country...Slavery in time will not be a speck in our country."

Pinkney can't let this attack slide, and pulls out another old chestnut that survived well into the twentieth century — "If slavery be wrong, it is justified by the example of all the world. Look at Greece, Rome, and other ancient states...In all ages one half of mankind have been slaves. If the Southern states are let alone they will probably stop importations. I would vote for it. An attempt to take away the right will produce serious objections to the Constitution, which I wish to see adopted."

Just in case Virginia is wavering, he attacks directly, concluding that Virginia only wants to stop the slave trade because it has more slaves than it needs and will gain from the rise in value of those slaves if imports are stopped.

* * * * * * * * *

So the debate ebbed and flowed, sometimes pounding on the shores and threatening to destroy the Convention, sometimes seeping in undetected and polluting seemingly unrelated issues. Today's leaders must also remain alert and expose similar corrosive, insidious, and corrupting frames in their own team debates. The examples of convicted corporate executives illustrate the extremes of these destructive frames.

The Framers Defend Their 'Frames'

The debate roiled on until the delegates finally compromised on a truly bad decision. The Constitution would prohibit the government from doing anything about the slave trade until 1808, twenty years hence. In fact, the Constitution even prohibited any amendments that would tamper with the slave importation provision. In the state ratifying conventions, the issue of slavery would be examined again, using the same tired frames. Alexander Hamilton examined Articles III and IV of the proposed Constitution and...[22]

> ...explained in *The Federalist* No. 80, these twin citizenship clauses aimed at a common purpose – namely, the prevention of state discrimination against citizens of sister states. Free blacks were also plainly encompassed by Articles III and IV as originally understood. Several states in 1787 not only openly regarded free blacks as citizens, but also allowed them to vote on equal terms with white men and thereby wield a political privilege that even white women, though citizens, generally lacked...

> One of the critical clauses in Article IV...gave slave states an explicit guarantee that they lacked under the background legal rules in place in 1787 America. In trying to sell the Constitution to his fellow slave masters in Virginia, [James] Madison explained that, despite its linguistic indirection, the language governing 'service or labour' was 'expressly inserted, to enable owners of slaves to reclaim them. This is a better security than any that now exits.'

How could Madison pander to his fellow slave owners so blatantly? Madison's principle biographer claims:[23]

> Of all evils, however, none was for Madison more pregnant with danger, and more intractable, than that of Negro slavery. His conviction of its immorality, and its incongruity in a nation resting on the Declaration of Independence, had been formed early, and never slackened. His failure in the 1780s to free himself from

dependence on slave labor, and to secure a law for gradual abolition in Virginia, doomed him it seemed, to live within a system he abhorred...In retirement, Madison renewed his efforts to abolish slavery.

Though he insisted in 1819 that liberal principles and improved conditions made slaves much better off than they were before the revolution, their degraded status was nevertheless intolerable under a supposedly free government.

Madison was framed by his belief that the cultures, experiences, and prejudices of both whites and blacks would lead to conflict and make it impossible for them to live together after emancipation. Thomas Jefferson and he believed that money from the sale of western lands by the government could be used to compensate the slaves' former owners for their freedom. Both were active in a society that sought to free and resettle blacks, first in the West and then in Africa. As critics pointed out to Madison at the time, the scheme was designed to get rid of *all* blacks, including freemen, and most blacks did not want to be sent to Africa.

Madison stubbornly held onto the resettlement scheme. Despite his mental torments and recorded kind treatment of his own slaves, he freed none of them, even in his will. Washington did free his slaves in his will. Jefferson freed a handful of slaves in his will, his purported children by his slave, Sally Hemmings. The vast majority of Jefferson's and Madison's slaves were sold off after each man died in order to pay their enormous debts.

As contemporary leaders discussed their mistakes, some admitted they also stubbornly held on to a position for too long. This is a particularly insidious type of frame; it blocks the recognition of new facts that could shatter the existing frame and lead to a better decision more quickly. For example, Charles J's insistence that poor company results were due only to external economics blinded him to other considerations for a long time. He was entrenched. Luckily, he was open to challenges from his executive team members, who finally chipped away at his perceptual frame. After he finally viewed the internal performance problems as major contributors to poor results, he acted quickly and got the company back on track.

Finding Alternative 'Frames'

The delegates and leaders in the early years of the republic did have other options for action. Madison's former secretary and longtime friend, Edward Coles, witnessed Russian serfdom first hand, inspiring him to free his own slaves and take them to the free state of Illinois. He...

> ...gave each some land, and helped them become good farmers. Madison was pleased Coles pursued 'the true course' of providing for his Negroes' happiness as well as their freedom...Madison, on the other hand, 'lulled' as Coles put it, by a lifetime of existence with slavery, and without Coles' zealous faith in the ultimate equality of the races, was unwilling to undertake the suffering and disruption, for him and his slaves, of individual manumission...That a man of Madison's realism and integrity should in this instance adhere to such an insufficient and compromised program is painful evidence of the virtually insoluble dilemma slavery posed for him...
>
> He withdrew from his intention, promised to Edward Coles, to free his slaves in his will...Learning of Madison's hesitation, Coles wrote urging him not to let the practical difficulties of manumission deter him from an act of freedom that would be 'the consummation of your glory'...A lifetime of opposition to slavery had thus been reduced in Madison's will to a gesture [that none

could be sold without their own consent and that of Dolley Madison]. Even that pledge was not honored.[24]

The framers and early leaders of the republic had another practical, realistic option. They could have expanded the Northwest Ordinance that prohibited slavery in all federal territories.[25]

In 1787, such a plan could probably have garnered significant Southern support...In 1784, Thomas Jefferson proposed that slavery be excluded from *all* Western lands after 1800, a plan that the Confederation Congress failed to pass because of the health-related absence of a single delegate...[George Mason, who condemned slavery so vehemently in the Convention,] in the ratification period railed against anything that might precipitate the immediate abolition of slavery in places where it had become entrenched...

Another approach, advocated years too late by Philadelphia delegate Rufus King, would have limited the three-fifths bonus to the original thirteen states... Elbridge Gerry, a Philadelphia delegate (and Declaration signer) who opposed the completed Constitution, floated a version of this idea [using proceeds from Western land sales to compensate owners of emancipated slaves] in the First Congress, and Rufus King publicly revived the concept in the aftermath of the Missouri Compromise in 1820. Madison himself privately endorsed a similar plan in 1819, when he focused directly on the issue of slavery in the West.

Bold Solutions Break the Frames

Another option carried efforts like Edward Cole's initiative even further. Robert Carter III was a member of the influential Carter family of Virginia, and one of the wealthiest of the Virginia elite. He owned a very large number of slaves distributed over many farms and plantations.

In 1791 he walked into the Northumberland District Courthouse and recorded a "deed of gift," thus performing an act of personal courage unequaled by his contemporaries or those who came after him. Obscured by the language of the eighteenth century, it was an elaborate plan to free every one of his over four hundred fifty slaves over a period of years. He freed "more American slaves than any other American slaveholder had ever freed, more American slaves than any American slaveholder would *ever* free."[26]

His name seldom appears among the notables listed as the founding fathers. He was neither a prominent legislator nor a participant in the Revolution or the framing of the Constitution. He did not leave rich diaries of his inner thoughts and outer deeds. He signed none of the great documents of the period. Although he was initially ambivalent about the Revolution, he became a convincing patriot. When mentioned at all, he is often confused with other Robert Carters in his wide-ranging clan.

He grew into his beliefs as part of the Great Awakening, the spiritual revival that swept the U.S. at the end of the eighteenth century. He began a spiritual and religious quest that led him to a variety of spiritual expressions and dissenting religions. He translated that belief into extraordinary action. In one of the churches where he was active, he associated freely with blacks, some free and some still enslaved. The congregation perceived the blacks as completely equal human beings and made them part of the church's decision-making structure.

He set in motion the largest emancipation of slaves prior to the Emancipation Proclamation [1863]. He was roundly criticized by his contemporaries, ridiculed for his sometimes peculiar beliefs, and ostracized by the Virginia elite. He didn't care. Carter took what he believed to be the right action. He encapsulated his position succinctly, "My plans and advice have never been pleasing to the world."[27]

Madison and others were certainly aware of what he was doing, but there is no evidence they corresponded or discussed it. Carter's elaborate emancipation plan resembled the plans in Northern states that freed slaves gradually. As the laws in the South concerning freeing slaves tightened in the late1890s, Carter accelerated his plan and all of his slaves went free, most with land and the support to survive on their own. In another important difference from Madison's resettlement plan, Carter did not require the freed people to leave Virginia or even the neighborhood.

George Washington, Carter's neighbor, decided to free his slaves and prepared a new will during 1799, the last year of his life. It was the culmination of a long, well-chronicled journey from holding the traditional views of racial inferiority of blacks to a more egalitarian perspective.[28] As Washington lay dying, he insisted that his instructions be carried out to the letter.

Like Washington, Robert Carter III simply took action on his beliefs. Unlike Washington, he was willing to face the personal economic disruption and social approbation of breaking the slave system and freeing his slaves in his lifetime. Because Carter believed in absolute human equality, he saw no need to transport the freed people somewhere else. He lived side by side with some of his former bondsmen.

Benjamin Franklin also overcame his eighteenth-century frames and changed his views on race. He started as an owner of a few slaves, and wrote pamphlets expressing the view that blacks were inferior. He evolved into something quite different.

> Franklin's conversion culminated in 1787, when he accepted the presidency of the Pennsylvania Society for Promoting the Abolition of Slavery...[A]t the Constitutional Convention...knowing the delicate compromise being made between North and South, he kept silent on the issue. After that, however, he became

outspoken...[Countering the fear of seven hundred thousand freed slaves entering a total population of four million] his abolition society dedicated itself not only to freeing slaves but also to helping them become good citizens...On behalf of the society, Franklin presented a formal abolition petition to Congress in February 1790.[29]

The Insidiousness of Frames

As Luda Kopeikina documents so convincingly in her research on executive decision-making,[30] because so many of our psychological frames are deeply embedded, they are invisible to us. These powerful frames prevent us from even seeing their existence. Madison's slavery frames deftly guided his behaviors from a secret hiding place deep within his psyche. Even his monumental intellect could not discover the frames.

When Franklin's petition to the first Congress to end slavery set off a firestorm from Deep South representatives, Madison quietly made sure it was bottled up in committee and tabled, just as he did with a similar petition from the Quakers. Madison, in the grip of his frames, rationalized these measures would not pass and would only inflame passions. He did not want to be associated with a doomed piece of legislation. Once again, his political frames triumphed over leadership.

Of course, Madison was not the only leader so deafened by his frames that he could not hear the frame-destroying arguments swirling around.

> [Patrick] Henry, moreover, raised the question that has long perplexed historians: how could the generation that produced the Declaration of Independence, declaring as it did the equality of all men, have done so little about the problem of slavery? Writing in 1773...Henry asked, 'Is it not amazing that at a time, when the rights of humanity are defined and understood with precision,

in a country, above all others, fond of liberty, that such an age and in such a country we find men...adopting a principle as repugnant to humanity, as it is inconsistent with the bible, and destructive to liberty?'

...As the author, in the Virginia Declaration of Rights, of the assertion that 'all men are created equally free and independent,' [George] Mason would have been as well suited as anyone to answer Henry's question. Unfortunately, the surviving records yield little direct evidence of how Mason reconciled, in his own mind, his commitment to freedom and democracy, his antipathy toward slavery, and his ownership of dozens [over two hundred] of black slaves.[31]

Mason, like the leading proponents of liberty for "all men," had complex frames, including their views of blacks and race, the nature and value of labor, and the role of government. These frames "served to limit his capacity to deal effectively with the problem of slavery...[T]hey do offer some clues to the origins of Mason's ambiguous legacy."[32] While Mason and others were often appalled by the blatant cruelty and violence shown toward slaves, they also believed blacks were only suited for manual labor, not intellectual development or social equality.

Although Mason later condemned slavery as a violation of the human rights of American blacks and Africans, his first public attack on the institution focused on its effect on Virginia's development on white morality. In the debate over slavery, the interests of blacks never, during Mason's lifetime, became paramount. Black rights were always weighed against, and diluted by, concerns about the interests of white society. Prejudice against blacks ran too deep for it to be otherwise... Hostility toward slavery, in reality, stemmed in part from a hostility toward blacks, which in turn crippled the antislavery cause. Racial prejudice worked to perpetuate American slavery, even if it was not essential to sustain the institution.[33]

Finally, these leaders were framed by the fact that slavery provided them a life where white owners could pursue their republican ideals. "Slavery allowed the planters to minimize their society's need for a large class of the working poor and to exclude their African substitutes from civil society."[34]

Despite the actions of individuals in freeing slaves, collectively, the leaders of the late eighteenth and first half of the nineteenth centuries could not escape their complicated frames around the bondage of their fellow humans. By using

> ...the 20 percent of the population that was black... as pawns with no rights the white man was bound to respect...they committed one of the worst mistakes in American history...With hindsight, we can see that the Founding Fathers might have provided for the phasing out of slavery over a relatively long term, principally by confining it geographically. But they saw things, as we all do, according to their lights [frames,] and they acted on their own vision.
>
> And of course the irony of it all was that the South gave up power to the North because it expected it would soon be dominant anyway, and the North gave up slavery to the South because it thought it would die out anyway, and both were wrong. The final lesson, then, may be that institutions, once established, are not easily changed.[35]

Escaping Frames and Taking Action

Understanding psychological frames helps leaders understand where colossal mistakes come from, but does not excuse them. In the end, leaders are judged by the actions they take, the results they get, and how they handle bad decisions. They are not judged by their beliefs, their frames, or their mental agonies over complex, difficult decisions.

Bad decisions are inevitable, given our humanness. Making mistakes and learning from them is part of the development of a leader's character. Ben Baldanza, president of Spirit Airlines, expressed it this way:

> I think the key is to create forums and create communication and opportunities for people to share ideas — for people to make mistakes. I strongly believe that someone who doesn't make mistakes is someone who just isn't doing enough. You're going to make mistakes. We don't want people to make the same mistake twice, and we want people to learn from mistakes. But I think creating an environment where mistakes are accepted as a piece of growth, and change and new ideas are encouraged rather than squelched is important, especially in thinking about serving our customers.

Baldanza's understanding of the role mistakes have in developing leadership was echoed by most of the executives interviewed. Greg Swienton, CEO of Ryder System, quoted almost verbatim Ben Franklin's final speech to the Constitutional Convention to illustrate the importance of challenging our frames. Visualize Franklin in his eighties, overweight and crippled with a gout attack. He asks James Wilson to read his remarks, which are addressed directly to the handful of delegates who announced they would not sign the Constitution.

> I confess that I do not entirely approve this Constitution at present...[H]aving lived long, I have experienced many instances of being obliged...to change

opinions even on important subjects...[T]he older I grow, the more apt I am to doubt my own judgment and pay more respect to the judgment of others...I cannot help expressing a wish that every member of the convention who may still have objections to it, would ... doubt a little of his own infallibility...and put his name to this instrument.[36]

Franklin speaks down the centuries to leaders. Although the three reluctant delegates were not swayed that day,[37] Franklin captured a key element of great leaders. They all know they make bad decisions sometimes. They know they are fallible and question their frames.

Leaders like Robert Carter III and this book's modern examples show people *can* escape their frames if they decide to do it.

[Robert Carter's] example is enough to remind us that there existed men and women during the Revolutionary War who knew what was right and who did not lack the personal will to act upon that belief. The more one reads in the twenty-first century about someone such as Robert Carter, the more one feels a sense of fury and frustration that there were already men and women in Virginia in the 1780s prepared to surrender money and power to bring a dull end to the institution of slavery, and thus the whole thing – the Civil War, Jim Crow, the Ku Klux Klan, two hundred years of relentless bitterness and division – could have whimpered and died...He does not soothe us, excuse us, or help us explain ourselves...[He] forces us to consider whether there now exist similar men and women...[38]

There *are* such men and women today who escape their frames, know what is right, and have the personal will to act upon it. They admit to and learn from their mistakes. They encourage others to follow their examples and create a culture that can break frames. They are true leaders.

In 2004, *In Focus Magazine* recognized PBS&J and its CEO, John Zumwalt, with its Achievers Award. The award recognized the engineering firm's commitment to diversity and underscored the company's growing national recognition as a special place to work.[39]

Zumwalt's brand of leadership at PBS&J emphasized understanding personality diversity to achieve great decision making and results. Spurred by discussions with a local official, he began to look at ethnic and racial diversity in an innovative way. He asked a simple question, "Do we look like the community decision-makers where we have our installations?" He established no quotas, no artificial goals, and had no pressure from outside regulators. He simply led.

> I wanted to set an example. I diversified our board, and now we're diversifying our leadership and management. Other companies may look at diversity statistics, but we're in the results business. I think the best way to effect change is to start talking about it and emphasizing it a lot. People started hiring a more diverse staff on their own. We created a Diversity Advisory Council to facilitate our efforts. We went to diversity-focused engineering and municipal organizations to recruit. I won't be satisfied until diversity's a seamless part of our culture. We will not leave any deserving employee behind. We're putting a new face on our future.

What Distinguishes Great Leaders?

- ***How does a leader handle the bad decision?*** Great leaders acknowledge their mistakes personally. They do not fall back on the passive "mistakes were made" formula. Instead, they say, "I made a mistake." They accept the consequences of that bad decision.

- ***What does a leader do?*** Great leaders take personal responsibility, usually without a lot of fanfare. They take the next right action, no matter what others say or do. They move quickly to fix their errors.

- ***How does a leader show his beliefs?*** Great leaders act on their beliefs and are courageous role models for their convictions.

- ***How does a leader use a mistake?*** Great leaders learn from their mistakes and act differently in the future. They discover the frames leading them to the bad decision in the first place. They get more diverse perspectives on their future decisions.

- ***How does a leader confront his or her frames?*** Great leaders understand their own perceptions of the situation can cloud their decision making. They seek other opinions. They recognize they are framed, and work to stand outside their own frames and doubt their own infallibility.

- ***How does a leader help others to admit and correct mistakes?*** Great leaders understand humans make mistakes. They encourage risk-taking and do not automatically punish mistakes. They make sure people have the opportunity to learn and grow from mistakes and confront their own limiting frames.

Discovering and breaking their own frames are essential disciplines for successful contemporary leaders. Yet this is not enough to guarantee success. Even if hard-nosed analysis of reality, vision, mission, and plan are in place, and frames are minimized, every leader is confronted with the need to put the plan into action. How does the leader pull off the crucial translation of plan into results?

Article VI

Execution is Harder than Revolution

"It's the tactical execution of whatever you decide to do that is more important than a great strategy."
— *Greg Swienton, CEO, Ryder System*

As the Constitutional Convention ended, a crowd gathered to find out what had really been happening in the Pennsylvania State House behind closed doors, sealed windows, and tight-lipped delegates. According to James McHenry, a Maryland delegate, as soon as Benjamin Franklin emerged from the hall, "an anxious lady...accosted him immediately...What type of government, she asked, have you delegates given us? To which he replied, 'A republic, madam, if you can keep it.'"[1]

Franklin's words, "if you can keep it," sum up the challenges faced not only by the framers but also by all leadership teams after they put together a robust plan, and must make it work. The anti-Federalists, as those who opposed the proposed Constitution were called, began marshaling their forces immediately, especially in key states such as Virginia and New York. Rhode Island, which refused to send delegates, was unlikely to join the new union readily.

Most delegates at the Convention knew the new Constitution would not be adopted automatically. They had created a three-part strategy to increase the chances of passage. First, because some of the delegates were also state representatives in the Confederation Congress, they convinced that body to submit the Constitution directly to the states without debate, amendments, or comments. Second, in the body of the Constitution the delegates inserted the ratification requirement of approval by only nine states. They had learned their lesson from failing to ever get the unanimous approval required to change the Articles of Confederation. Third, the Convention delegates determined that each state would elect a special ratifying convention, rather than use the existing legislature. They knew the states would not give up their supreme power voluntarily. Executing these strategies was a major coup for the emerging Federalists.

In the first few months, the specially-called state ratifying conventions in Delaware, New Jersey, Connecticut, and Georgia agreed to the new Constitution with unanimous votes. Pennsylvania ratified with a hefty margin.[2] By the time the Massachusetts convention met, the opposition was ready to mount a strong campaign. Then the Rhode Island convention voted in March 1788, and defeated the Constitution by a whopping 2,708–237 vote. The count stood at six states for to one against the new Constitution. Tension was building. Virginia and New York weren't scheduled to vote until June and July.

During this period, James Madison and Alexander Hamilton, with a little help from an ailing John Jay, turned out the classic *Federalist Papers*, writing under the collective pseudonym, Publius.[3] Anonymous essays and pamphlets were a major component of political discourse in the late eighteenth century, comparable to our modern blogosphere.

> In this verbal Armageddon one bright champion of the new dispensation [Constitution] stood forth in armor of particular brilliance. He was 'Publius,' and he fought valiantly in the State of New York, where the issue was finely drawn and in doubt to the very last. This 'Publius' performed the Herculean task of publishing seriatim between October, 1787, and May, 1788, a total of eighty-five lengthy articles in defense of the New Constitution...[They] speedily attracted attention far beyond the borders of the State of New York.[4]

Today's savvy leaders know they need to build consensus ahead of time when they want to make a radical change in the organization. Like Hamilton and Madison, they marshal their best persuasive arguments and work ahead of time with team members, one at a time. Greg Swienton, CEO of Ryder System, remarked, "You have to find a way to warm up your audience, so when it comes time for them to make a decision, you've got them on your side."

Although scholars may debate the effect *The Federalist* had on the ratification process itself, the widely circulated essays reflect the debated issues in most of the ratifying conventions. The intensity of Madison and Hamilton's efforts indicates the hard work that was necessary to secure ratification. Chief Justice John Marshall encapsulated the value of *The Federalist* this way, "Its intrinsic merit entitles it to this high rank (as a complete commentary on our Constitution), and the part two of its authors performed in framing the Constitution, put it very much in their power to explain the views with which it was framed."[5] Later in life, Madison said that if people wanted to understand the original intent of the Constitution, they should look at the records of the debates in all the state ratifying conventions.

In April and May, Maryland and South Carolina respectively ratified, bringing the total to eight states for the new government. This charged atmosphere swirled around the Virginia and New York conventions as they began their deliberations. Hamilton and Madison, although only in their thirties, went into their respective state ratifying conventions and debated formidable, more politically experienced opponents. In New York, Hamilton faced off against powerful Governor George Clinton and his anti-Federalist allies, while Madison had to face down not only the most powerful political leader, Patrick Henry, but also the powerful moral leader, George Mason. Mason had been active at the Constitutional Convention until the last day, when he refused to sign the new document.

Until the last moment, both New York and Virginia were in the doubtful column. If either or both of these two large states failed to ratify, the stability of any future union was in jeopardy. Then, on June 21, 1788, New Hampshire ratified, and the Constitution went into effect. On June 25, Virginia ratified by an 89–79 vote and New York followed suit on July 26 with a paper-thin 30–27 margin.

The Union of States existed and the Confederation government was no more. Now the leaders turned their attention to creating a new government and implementing their plan. George Washington was unanimously elected President of the new republic. Hamilton became Secretary of the Treasury. Madison went into the House of Representatives after his appointment to the Senate was blocked by a vindictive Patrick Henry.

In November 1789, North Carolina ratified and joined the Union while Rhode Island held out until May of 1790, finally ratifying by a vote of 34 to 32.[6] Execution was indeed harder than Revolution.

Innovation Drives the Execution Curve

Today, strong teams usually come up with a robust plan and face the same sort of worries as the framers: 'Can we get everyone to accept the plan, and can we actually get the results we planned?' The value of the plan is in the results the team achieves. The leader's responsibility is to communicate the plan to everyone in the organization, and make sure everyone understands how his job fits into achieving the planned results.

Modern leaders demonstrate the same tenacity as the framers in seeing their plans come to life. Steve Hayworth, CEO of Gibraltar Private Bank and Trust Company, oversaw implementation of the bank's strategic plan to grow the bank assets from $40 million to over $1 billion in just over eleven years.[7] The bank used its strategic planning process to help the company make the crucial transition from entrepreneurial start-up to established, growing corporation without creating a lumbering bureaucracy, and used joint departmental goals to drive teamwork.[8]

When the Gibraltar leadership team created its first strategic plan, a senior executive suggested appointing task masters to establish clear authority for each element. For example, at this point there was no executive human resources officer. Another executive stepped forward as the point person to report on staff morale and oversee an employee engagement survey. Holding someone responsible for each goal may seem obvious, but many companies fail to execute this critical step.

The bank's second innovation was to insist on "managing on the top page." Previously, when the leadership team met, they spent most of their time delving into operational details within various departments. Now they focused their discussions on company-wide goals and their progress towards these. Their deliberations were around what, if any, action they needed to take based on bank-wide results. These results were presented in a one-page spreadsheet, and arranged according to the strategic plan goals and objectives. Every meeting agenda was constructed around these goals, objectives, and results.

Gibraltar's third innovation was to adopt the notion that "the plan is the boss." This reminded them to stay focused; they could not add new initiatives or drop existing ones without considering in great detail how the action would affect overall results. When the unexpected happened, such as a drop in interest rates, the bank could respond thoughtfully and strategically.

Each department developed a plan based on the bank's Top Page plan, creating action plans to get results that supported the bank's objectives. As each successive level tackled the planning process, something remarkable happened. People became excited about setting their own objectives. For example, in one department, the staff came back with a plan to increase revenue by $15 million. Their executive cautioned them to be more "realistic," and set a goal of only $2 million.

But the staff was insistent. The team met their robust goal in six months. Most people will expect more of themselves than any boss would dare to ask.

Make Results Real

When the Gibraltar Private leadership team entered the sunlit conference room for the second meeting after the initial plan was launched, they found their accustomed places, sipped their coffee, and chatted quietly. They looked around for the usual financial reports with their neat rows, columns, and numbers, but they couldn't find them. Then Hayworth entered the room and immediately turned the meeting over to CFO Tony Caron.

Caron flipped a switch, and a jumbo flat screen flickered to life. The first slide set the tone with a quote from a business book the team had been reading — another of the bank's innovations. One by one, the goals and objectives flashed on the screen. A colorful graph illustrated each one, its current status, and historical data if available.

People sat forward in their seats, coffee growing cold. Engaged, and even mesmerized by what they were seeing, they began to grasp the meaning behind the data in a new way. They saw the clear trends over time, not just individual data points. Occasionally there were little gasps or sighs as a particularly dramatic graph appeared.

With that simple PowerPoint demonstration, Caron helped the seasoned, entrepreneurial bankers experience the results of their work in a new way. They could no longer simply seize on a high or low number — "Why are the commercial loans down this month?" — and question it at a tactical level. The numbers were now placed in context. For example, the trends over the past year for commercial loans were apparent, so the most recent month's result was not a red flag, but simply one data point among many when presented in context.

Targets are Just Targets

As the Gibraltar leadership team looked at results in this context over the next months, they started using another new phrase, "targets are just targets." They realized that sometimes the targets they set were realistic, and sometimes they weren't. They moved from being judgmental about results to being more analytical. They started asking new questions: "What's the root cause?" "Did we set the target too high or too low?" "What do we need to do to get back on track?" Several years into adopting strategic planning and execution, the CEO and CFO report:

Hayworth: You have to remember, we're a bunch of bankers. We're numbers people. We're used to saying the numbers look 'good' or the numbers look 'bad.' We had to change our thinking, and not get too hung up on the numbers and avoid judgment about the data. Instead, we started trying to understand what the numbers were telling us. What were the trends? If the numbers were perfect every time, maybe we needed to measure something else. The judgment we needed to make was, 'Are we moving in the right direction? Is this information helpful at all, just because we're tracking it? Is it still relevant?'

Caron: We realized these data are nothing more than the results of tactics that we implemented to achieve our overall objectives. As a corporation, that's how we're looking at them. We're not pointing fingers. We're just trying to understand, to have knowledge, to get better. Are we tracking the right things? Are things moving in the right direction?

Today, we have coalesced around four goals and four or five objectives underneath each goal. We are going to make the tactics to achieve those objectives work as best we can.

Hayworth: I think it's down at the lower levels of the organization where planning is having the most impact. These folks are participating in the planning process and they understand what their contributions are and how they are valued. The strategic planning process is a great way to engage and empower everybody in the company.

It doesn't mean that everybody is going to buy in out of the gate. When people's opinions count, there is going to be debate about what's in the best interest of the company; not the best interest of the CEO or the best interest of the department. They've gained a perspective on the best interest of this thing called the corporate entity.

As the bank's implementation of the plan continued and the improved results in many areas came rolling in, more people became aware this strategic approach worked.

As mentioned earlier, Hayworth led discussions of popular business book chapters at each monthly meeting. Those ongoing discussions were lively and added yet another dimension to the executives' thinking. They developed a common vocabulary and started applying the various authors' insights to their situations as they expanded their perception frames.[9] The framers, with their extensive reading in history and political philosophy, spoke in shorthand about details of the Roman Republic, and expected everyone to understand their references and their application to the matter at hand. Gibraltar's leadership team could do the same with the shared experience of their business reading.

Executing in Bad Times

Then interest rates dropped precipitously. Suddenly, the lucrative lines of the bank's business declined, threatening to derail the bank's stunning progress as competition became more fierce. As the executive team gathered for the monthly meeting, there was a palpable anxiety in the room. Visions of axes falling danced in people's heads. Everyone had seen the papers. There was little banter or small talk. There was no way to sugarcoat it. The numbers were going to be bad. Competitors were looking for new gimmicks to stay afloat and running incoherent ads for strange new products. Despite the bright sunshine outside the floor-to-ceiling windows, it was gloomy.

Hayworth and Caron entered. When Hayworth spoke, he said things were a little tight and might get tighter but, because they had embarked on implementing their strategic plan, they were in relatively good shape. In fact, if they adjusted a few targets and emphasized certain products over others, they would pull through. Hayworth said the board agreed, and would continue to support them in their innovative efforts. "The plan is the boss" was still the guiding principle, along with the proviso "targets are just targets." As Hayworth turned the meeting over to Caron for the monthly data evaluation, the dark cloud in the room began to dissipate. Everyone visibly relaxed.

Not only did Gibraltar survive the economic calamity while several other banks went out of business, but it also continued to grow, doubling staff and profits over a four-year period. In many ways, Gibraltar's experience parallels that of the early republic and the new Constitution. The internal weaknesses and external threats had not magically disappeared. With a strong, three-branched government in place, the country was in a position to *respond* strategically to each crisis. The government could focus the collective intelligence of a wide variety of people to come up with viable solutions. At Gibraltar, the leadership team used their strategic plan to focus their collective intelligence on facing the latest business crisis strategically, rather than *reacting* tactically and unsuccessfully, as some other banks were doing.

Strategy Focuses Growth

Gibraltar continued innovating. Steve Hayworth transformed the traditional human resources function to help management teams at every level, including the executive team, prepare and monitor their plans. Employees' performance evaluation included a planning activities and results section. And as Gibraltar expanded into new markets, planning evolved to be more market centric, with an eye on growth in each unique area.

Gibraltar's goals have settled into a Balanced Scorecard approach with emphasis on financials, internal processes, employees, and clients. Perhaps one of the most innovative parts of Gibraltar's evolution has been in the area of its clients. Gibraltar's target market is "high net-worth individuals," and the bankers understood the importance of working with the family, not just the individual client. Gibraltar bankers decided to try something unique. They engaged families in a strategic planning process, which closely mirrored their corporate planning processes. The bankers understood all too well the traditional "shirt sleeves to shirt sleeves in three generations" story that played itself out in wealthy families. Hayworth and Caron elaborate:

> **Hayworth:** Today we talk about 'wealth creators' and 'legacy families.' It has really evolved over the last few years. We've become interested in the generational transfer of wealth. Did you know that, in over seventy percent of the instances where family wealth is created, it's completely gone by the third generation? If I'm the first-generation wealth creator and I've demonstrated that I'm pretty good at making money for the betterment

and enjoyment of my family, I may never have heard anyone tell me I'm at risk about that continuing.

Caron: We created a special department with the freedom to go outside and look at resources to support our clients and their families. We are a resource in the area of family meetings. Why should they even think about a family meeting? What are the pros and cons? What are the different ways to conduct a family meeting and construct an agenda? Do they need us to facilitate?

We don't charge a fee for this. It creates a deep relationship, because no one else is doing this. Other new things are coming out of this planning with the families. We're considering building a philanthropy program for children. Clients said to us, 'I'm worried about what the effect of our financial success is on my children.' With privilege comes responsibility. Building collaborative decision-making models for the descendants of a successful family will serve that family for future generations.

Hayworth: The banker can really help the wealth creator look at things differently. The clients don't see the pitfalls until they're in the middle of them. What parent wants to see the family unravel that way? We want to create an environment where we are providing a resource to help them acknowledge that there is the potential for destructive forces in the family's financial success.

We help them frame their future and decide what they need to do to have that future. We get them thinking about balance and what they want. We help them get in control by building a framework they can use. Then we help them create a family mission. It's a powerful statement for a family.

Caron: The strategic planning process has helped us mature enough within our own organization to realize that we're not transaction-based anymore as a result of this strategic thinking. Our evolution accelerated when we started the strategic planning process, because so many of our initiatives have come out of that initial SWOT analysis.

Hayworth: This approach gives our clients a way to make decisions about what to invest in and when. We help them understand the quantitative and qualitative building blocks of wealth. There is a purpose and a process. Just like the bank, the family is really creating a strategic plan, with goals and tactics and execution. They're meeting periodically to review and evaluate progress. When big events happen, we ask, 'How does that affect your plan?' It helps remove emotion from the decision making as much as possible.

Tony is absolutely right. We have moved away from being a transactional company and created a powerful process that is going to be a distinguishing characteristic of our relationship company.

One of the long-range goals that Gibraltar set was to ally itself with a compatible company as a way to grow and expand the business. In 2005, it reached this goal by becoming an affiliate partner of a respected wealth management public holding company, which operates as a loose confederacy of independent businesses that are in allied fields. Hayworth was determined to maintain the integrity of Gilbraltar and its values as he sought a partner. In the end, relentless execution of the strategic plan paid off in Gibraltar's stellar financial growth.

Execution Means Tough Decisions

The description of how Gibraltar Private Bank and Trust went through its plan implementation focused primarily on how the leaders made things work. Of course, Gibraltar hit bumps in the road; Hayworth faced tough decisions. Like Madison, Hamilton, and the other delegates to the Constitutional Convention, modern leaders must leave their planning sessions and face the realities of implementation. The framers had to fight for ratification, enter the new government, and fight to make the Constitution a reality. The strategic leader cannot float above the fray. He must make those tough decisions and then make sure they are implemented.

Michael Howe, former CEO of MinuteClinic, articulated what almost every leader who was interviewed reported.

> The hardest decisions for me will always be about people. I love the recruiting, I love interviewing, I love figuring out who's going to fit and who's not. It's always tough on the other side when you have to cut someone loose. I had a great mentor who told me, 'You never fire anyone too soon.' It just sounds so cold until you really think about it. It's funny, but I've had so many good experiences where I have terminated someone's employment.
>
> The very first time I fired somebody was at Proctor and Gamble. It was a very acrimonious separation. Ten years later, I was in a hotel lobby and I heard this voice calling to me. I turned around and the man looked at me and said, 'Michael, I've wanted to talk to you for years.' And I'm thinking, 'Oh, no.' He said, 'Man, I was so wrong. Thank you! It was the best thing that ever happened to me. I didn't like what I was doing and it pushed me into something I absolutely love.' It goes back to the issue of culture and where people fit. He didn't fit where he was

and he did fit the culture where he ended up.

Yet tough decisions can be exciting. As Howe grew Minute Clinic from nineteen to over five hundred installations, he was working in uncharted territory.

One of the things that appealed to me was this is very much like the founding fathers. Nobody has gone before us. It's totally ambiguous. And that's exciting! We get to write the rules. I think that's why we're so effective. No one could stand up and say, 'Well, we've done it and here's the stake in the ground and here's what's happened.' There are no idea killers.

You do have to have vision. You do have to have the willingness to let everybody exercise their gifts, because you don't know where you're going. You don't have all the answers. So the best thing to do is pose a lot of questions and see what happens.

Howe took inspiration from the founders to help him in what he calls his "minor microcosm event. I think the fact that no one had done this — created a country, created a society from the ground up — was unique. They had these multiple agendas that had to be blended into one. And they came together with the sole purpose of creating that society, creating that civilization."

For John Zumwalt, one of his toughest decisions came when he was still COO at PBS&J. The company had grown by acquisition during the 1990s. He realized the culture seemed to be weakening and that he had "an organizational chart of companies, not people."

Just as the framers had to find a way to convert thirteen distinct states into one nation, Zumwalt had to unify seven diverse companies into one.

The biggest risk I took was standing back and saying, 'This doesn't look great. Why don't we consolidate all of these companies?' Of course, all of them had different cultures. We thought, 'Let's give them all a single mission and future and combine all the financials, the entire infrastructure, and have a single purpose for everybody moving forward.'

Zumwalt's board challenged him to consolidate without changing profitability "one iota." That was the break he needed, because no one knew what an iota was. Zumwalt began implementing his decision and knitting the seven companies together, uniting them under a single mission. "That was not without pain. A couple of directors from the acquired firms didn't want anything to do with my 'oneness' program and they left. We had to sell one of the companies that didn't want to be part of the new unified mission."

At the same time, with the Y2K computer bug looming, PBS&J switched over to new computer systems for finance, accounting, human resources, and more. "We kind of threw the whole company up in the air in 1999 and saw how it was going to come down. The good news is, it came down well. By the next year, we started to take off and have been growing revenues dramatically every since. I didn't know that I couldn't do it, so why not do it?"

After Greg Swienton's leadership team comes up with a new strategic plan for Ryder System, they focus on communicating the strategic direction. The team members explain why they are going in the new direction to build understanding and acceptance, just as the framers did in *The Federalist* and hundreds of other publications and private correspondence. But as Swienton explains,

> Those strategic plans have to get translated into a tactical execution plan. It's one thing to say, 'this is a market we want to go after.' It's another to say, 'Who's going

to do it? Who's going to sell it? Who's going to test it? Who's going to launch it?' That's when you get into the details. I'm a great believer in the concept that it is not the greatest, most elegant strategies that are successful. It's the tactical execution of whatever you decide to do that is more important than a great strategy.

The business sector is not the only part of the economy that requires strategic leadership to navigate organizational transformation. David Brown, as city manager of Coral Gables, Florida, had to guide the city through major changes and make arduous decisions.[10] He began his association with the city of Coral Gables, Florida as a summer lifeguard. Many years later, in 1986, he returned as an assistant city manager.

The City Beautiful, as it is called, has forty-four thousand residents, an international business community, and cultural prowess. Established in 1925 by George Merrick, the city's design and Mediterranean character were influenced by the Garden City movement founded in 1898 by Sir Ebenezer Howard. The philosophy was to create planned, self-contained cities surrounded by greenbelts that balanced residences with industry and agriculture.

In 2001, Brown became city manager. For much of his seven-year tenure, the major challenge Brown faced was to protect the city's quality of life. In 2004, after increased crime began to dominate the agenda, Brown selected a new police chief, Michael Hammerschmidt.

Hammerschmidt was a thirty-two-year veteran police officer with a master's degree in public administration, well-known in the law enforcement community as an innovator. He focused on two major initiatives to reduce crime, community programs and strategic operations. For example, he put more foot patrols into the reviving downtown area and residential neighborhoods. He set high goals for responsiveness and upgraded the 9-1-1 communication center technology to support them. The results of these efforts were significant decreases in overall crime and response time to emergency calls.[11]

With crime reduced, traffic and congestion took center stage with the public, along with the more threatening prospect of unbridled growth, which could destroy the unique character of the city. Yet Brown perceived a more insidious challenge – response time. The city needed to respond more quickly to the needs of both the residents and businesses.

"Survival had to do with automation. We were not going to survive unless we got out of the nineteenth century," he said. Brown put the city on an aggressive path of computer systems modernization, and tackled the revision of outdated city codes.

> So we took the bull by the horns and upgraded all of our computer systems and networks and installed new enterprise software. At the same time we rewrote the zoning code, the city charter, the procurement code, the comprehensive land use plan, and the municipal codes, all in two years. Nobody does that.
>
> When we started the automation project, we realized we had to reengineer the way most employees have done their jobs for a long time. That wasn't easy. We had to jump a few hurdles, and we had a few bumps and bruises, but if we didn't do it now, five years from now we'd be very, very lost. We just couldn't keep up with the requests for information and service and the costs of both.
>
> The strategic planning process made us think three to five years down the road. We got the mayor and commissioners involved in setting goals for our future. Then, all the departments created their plans for growth. We made those plans happen.

As department after department became part of the integrated computer system, citizens could access information online, contractors could do much of their permitting work through the automated system, and financial controls finally had some rigor. "In the old days, we were forty-five days behind in knowing what had happened with our spending. You could actually spend in a deficit way because you weren't caught up. At midyear, we had to sit down and go through, department by department, to balance it all out. With the new system we could click a button, and if the money's not there, the system won't let you spend!"

Brown's farsightedness in pushing the city toward greater automation paid off on many levels. As his last message on the City's new website read, "In the last six years, the City has not dealt with quick fixes, but began building strategies...for the long-term. The foundation is ready to take this City to a new level and into the 21st Century."

Brown was not just being optimistic; he had some hard data to back him up. Despite all the regulatory and automation changes, the city did not lose sight of its focus on historic restoration and capital improvements. When Brown began his stint as city manager, the reserve funds were only $600,000. Within six years, he grew them to a record-breaking $7 million, improving the city's bond rating to AA1. The leadership team set a longer range goal of a bond rating of AAA, with ten percent of the operating budget in unencumbered reserves.

For the department directors, finally having a concrete plan for the future meant both stronger results and less pain at budget time. They went into discussions with the finance director and Brown with clear plans, priorities, and the ability to defend their plans. This also helped Brown as he went to the city commission for the annual budget authorization. "In the past, we never tied our work plan to a set of goals and objectives approved by the commission. At budget time, it was willy-nilly at best. Now our plan is tied to each one of those goals or objectives. We built a documented financial trail. It allowed us to sit down and measure exactly what we accomplished on the previous year's goals. Then we could send that information out to the citizens and show them what we did with their money."

Finally, Brown pointed out that the new approach to budgeting and planning resulted in greater team building.

> Before, it was cut, cut, cut. In the new system, department directors brought in their work plans and when we didn't have the money to cover everything, we went through it as a group. They knew that we could move resources around if we had to. They worked better as a team when they saw that they might lose some one year, but get it back the following year. The department directors could defend their budgets because they were based on their work plans and the goals set by the commission. The commission's goals were all in the budget.

The constant push for improving every aspect of city government and the lives of residents, businesses, and visitors, was recognized in 2005 by the Florida League of Cities when Brown was chosen the Florida Cities of Excellence Award's City Manager of the Year.

Not long after this interview, Florida revised its property tax rates and distribution of revenues to local governments. Like other municipalities, Coral Gables was hit hard. Brown and the city commission were forced to make painful decisions. Because the city government had a planning infrastructure in place, it did not wield the budget-cutting ax as the blunt instrument that many unprepared cities and counties used. Because of Brown's decision to upgrade the technology infrastructure, the city realized major operational savings. Despite the expense of the upgrades, the actual information technology services budget fell by $2 million, and five years later was still $1 million less that the pre-consolidation costs. The percent of the entire budget devoted to technology was also reduced from 5.4 percent to 3.1 percent. Brown and the city did not escape the pain of budget cuts, but they did escape the chaos. Once again, strategic leadership was crucial for making tough decisions.

The 'Madison Factor'

Execution does not just happen. In many organizations, there are specific individuals who take on the job of shepherding the planning and execution processes. Often, this responsibility is not part of their official job description. They believe in the promise of the process, and set out to make it yield results. Of course, no one person can do it alone. Yet these influential people, who often work behind the scenes, make the difference between converting the leader's vision into reality — or not. It is hard to imagine the early republic without the powerful leadership of George Washington. Yet, just as important in many ways was the "mighty little Madison."

Fathering the Constitution: Getting the Father of His Country on Board

Throughout the winter and spring of 1786-87, correspondence flew among the principle conspirators who instigated the Constitutional Convention — General George Washington, James Madison, Alexander Hamilton, Gouverneur Morris, Benjamin Franklin, John Jay, and others. They agreed that governance under the Articles of Confederation was a shambles; in their words, it lacked "energy." They believed the Union was doomed to disintegrate without radical action.

They took action by bringing pressure on their legislators and representatives in the Confederation Congress. Although the Confederation Congress did sanction the Convention, calling the meeting didn't mean people would actually show up. The presence of General Washington, who had achieved iconic status and was almost universally admired and respected, would be crucial. Without him to lend political cover, many leaders simply would not come.

Yet the Constitutional Convention needed Washington as more than a figurehead. He was an advocate of strong central government, republican ideals, and abhorred the chaos into which the Congress and warring, self-centered states were leading the country. Washington had spent a lifetime carefully grooming his image and reputation. This Convention was a risky business. Could he afford to be associated with a failure?

Madison was relentless. Imagine the two of them in Washington's parlor, the diminutive, Madison and the tall, athletic Washington, talking late into the night. Picture them at their writing tables, penning letters to one another with the frequency of today's e-mail or text messages. Of course, Madison was not alone in badgering Washington; eventually, the collective pressure worked. Madison had already engineered Washington's appointment to the Virginia delegation.

Fathering the Virginia Plan

Madison was a skilled politician, fired in the crucible of Virginia politics and the Continental Congress. He had already enlisted the help of his neighbor and friend, Thomas Jefferson. Jefferson sent him hundreds of books from Paris on government from "ancient to modern," as Madison characterized them. Madison combined that knowledge with a lifetime of studying and working in government. His interest in political philosophy began in his days as a student at the College of New Jersey (now Princeton University) under the guidance of Scottish Enlightenment scholar John Witherspoon. In fact, Madison had been the college's first graduate student before returning to Virginia to enter the political fray.

With his raw intelligence and analytical powers, Madison digested histories and treatises and developed his plan for the new Constitution. He got suggestions from colleagues around the country and sketched out his plan to Washington in order to gain his support. Washington, while not a scholar, had clearly articulated views on the need for a strong, national, republican government that agreed with Madison's plan.

To set his plan in motion, Madison showed up in Philadelphia early, getting to know the arriving delegates and polishing his draft. He worked with the Virginia delegates as they arrived and solicited their final ideas and agreement. He persuaded Edmund Randolph, the governor of Virginia and host of the Convention, to present this "Virginia Plan" at the first official session. Madison had maneuvered all the pieces into place and was prepared to put on the final push for a new Constitution.

Fathering the Record

During the Convention, Madison was a dynamo. He worked the floor, spoke on every issue, and took lengthy notes. Not content with the official record of decisions, he used his own shorthand to capture much of what was said and then transcribed his notes each night. It is largely through Madison's notes that we have a detailed record of what happened. He believed the world needed to know exactly how a republican constitution is created. Madison's own words describe the picture vividly as he did the job that he said nearly killed him.

> The curiosity I had felt during my researches into the History of the most distinguished Confederacies...and the deficiency I found...in what related to the process, the principles, the reasons, & the anticipations... determined me to preserve as far as I could an exact account of what might pass in the Convention...[for] future curiosity by an authentic exhibition of the objects, the opinions, & the reasonings from which the new System of Govt was to receive its peculiar structure & organization. Nor was I unaware of the value of such a contribution to the fund of materials for the History of

a Constitution on which would be staked the happiness of a people great even in its infancy, and possibly the cause of Liberty throughout the world.

...In pursuance of the task I had assumed I chose a seat in front of the presiding member, with the other members on my right & left hands. In this favorable position for hearing all that passed, I noted in terms legible & in abbreviations & marks intelligible to myself what was read from the Chair or spoken by the members; and losing not a moment unnecessary between the adjournment & reassembling of the Convention I was enabled to write out my daily notes during the session or within a few finishing days after its close in the extent and form preserved in my own hand on my files...It happened also that I was not absent a single day nor more than a casual fraction of an hour in any day, so that I could not have lost a single speech, unless a very short one.[12]

Fathering the Constitution

Madison rejected the notion that he was the Father of the Constitution, insisting that "This was not, like the fabled Goddess of Wisdom, the offspring of a single brain. It ought to be regarded as the work of many heads & many hands."[13] Although many of Madison's original ideas did not make it into the final document, he is still rightfully referred to as its "father" because of his unstinting work in the Constitution's creation and implementation.

The twin sources of Madison's strength as he entered the Constitutional Convention were his whole-souled intellectual preparation to cope with the profound questions of how to establish a strong but free constitutional government, and his mastery, acquired through more than a decade of experience with Virginia and continental affairs, of the multitudinous aspects of representing the people as a legislator in a critical era of revolutionary upheaval.[14]

Modern teams also need someone with a similar commitment to push the pieces into place, pull together the existing situational analysis, talk up the planning process, and make sure the important details from the session are captured and distributed. The innovative leader cannot devote the time to becoming the expert on the details. Many successful teams have a "Madison Factor," a person who believes strongly in the initiative and fosters it with the other executives, and pushes for full adoption. The contemporary "Madisons" wield influence through their ability to persuade others, just as the original did.

Fathering Virginia's Ratification

When the Constitution was signed and sent to the states by Congress, the fight was not over. Once again, Madison sprang into action. With Alexander Hamilton and John Jay, he wrote the great political treatise and argument for the new Constitution, *The Federalist*. Then, he went into the Virginia ratifying convention and faced down one of his longtime and most fierce opponents, Patrick Henry, as well his own frail health.

Perhaps because of his exertions at the Convention and his gargantuan efforts in *The Federalist*, Madison suffered a devastating attack of the "bilious indisposition" that plagued him throughout his life. Some days he was too weak to leave his bed, while on others, he had to beat an embarrassing retreat from the floor.

Imagine the frail Madison in the packed meeting room, watching as Henry periodically took to the floor with his dramatic and pyrotechnic performances, seldom failing to move people to action. Yet Madison held his ground with his quiet, passionate, and persuasive style, systematically eviscerating Henry's arguments and bombast. See him standing there, holding his notes in his hat as he rises to speak. Or imagine him cornering delegates in the corridors and gaining their support, or bucking up the confidence of his allies. Even Edmund Randolph reversed his earlier refusal to support the new Constitution. Madison hammered away at the anti-Federalists until they were finally defeated by a ten-vote margin.[15]

Contemporary leaders who take on the Madison role must have stamina. Organizational change is never easy; entrenched interests are hard to dislodge. Those who see their self-interest embedded in the status quo often push back hard. The champion of the new may be in for a protracted battle.

Fathering the Bill of Rights

Madison was still not through. Although he did not believe a Bill of Rights was necessary,[16] he realized that a strong segment of the opposition to the new Constitution in many states, including Virginia, had come from the demand for such a statement. With Randolph and others pushing for another convention,[17] Madison agreed to sponsor amendments to the new Constitution as one of his first acts in the new Congress. In the new House of Representatives, he kept his word, consolidating the dozens of proposed amendments into a manageable number, and the first ten amendments, the Bill of Rights, passed the House and went to the states for speedy ratification.

Madison became Washington's point man in the House and fought for the legislation that made the new Government work. He was Washington's confidant, advising him on appointments, etiquette, and legislation, as well as ghostwriting speeches. He pulled his political magic to pass Alexander Hamilton's controversial finance plan. He served in Jefferson's cabinet, and followed him as President. In retirement, he continued to be a sought-after elder statesman; his views on the meaning of the Constitution were widely influential.

The *Madison Factor* at Gibraltar Private Bank

Throughout his long leadership career, George Washington sought out younger leaders to help make his ideas a reality. In Washington's first term as President, Madison served that critical function. Modern leaders often find such team members who can take initiative and set change in motion.

Steve Hayworth at Gibraltar Private Bank admires Washington as a leader because "he was fearless. I have to respect someone who was picked by a group of peers." Hayworth mirrors George Washington's style of leading from behind the scenes. He credits his CFO, Tony Caron, for seeing to it that the new strategic plan was implemented on a day-to-day basis. "I never once said to him, 'Would you lead this effort?' He took it upon himself to do that. He always makes decisions in the company's best interest."

Caron was one of the first members of the executive team to grasp the great power of the planning process. During the preparatory situational analysis, he pulled everyone's information together. At the planning session, he saw the team's SWOT analysis as a turning point for the bank.

On his own, he worked with each of the executives, steadily and persistently helping them gather and interpret their data. As Hayworth describes it:

> What was critical for us was the leadership Tony demonstrated. He was uniquely qualified, because he has so much respect in the organization. He's never been viewed as political. He can make a decision. His opinion, his decision, will be one that people will say, 'I understand why he's doing that. It's not personal.' It was his leadership and maturity that helped as we went through the [strategic planning and execution]

process. He became even more productive and critical for the company.

Like Madison, Caron took on the challenge of implementing organizational transformation, systematically brought people on board and kept up the momentum, all with his quiet, unassuming style.

Caron sees his role as building a framework for a disciplined approach to execute the company's vision. Once they dived into the SWOT analysis and created the plan, he found that "everyone got engaged in the ultimate goals and said, 'We can figure this out.'" As he began to look at everything in a new light, he brought in his next innovation, the dynamic, visual charting of the data, which helped people understand their progress even more clearly.

The *Madison Factor* at York Container

Remember York Container Company, the family-owned business in Pennsylvania that produces corrugated packaging and displays for regional manufacturers? Steve Tansey, son-in-law of one of the owners, began working at the company and learning the details of the business several years ago. He immediately embraced the strategic planning process the company was struggling to implement. He worked closely with all the departments to gather data and created the first dynamic, graphic displays of the results for the leadership team. For a time, he played the role of the *Madison factor*, working with many of the supervisors and managers to get their operations on the road to improvement.

When Tansey became COO, he used his own analytic and persuasive powers to build a new infrastructure of critical managers in sales, human resources, finance, customer service, technology, and production. He helped put new managers in key positions, and they became the *Madison factors* by energizing their employees, who became more engaged and productive. He worked with a consultant who functioned as the interim CFO to lay the groundwork for improved financial management as well as a transition to professional management. When the consultant was appointed as CEO, Tansey was in a position to build on a solid base of accomplishment. The revitalized leadership team made the company more competitive and profitable.

Tansey, in the tradition of Madison, takes virtually no credit for his hard work and great results. "While I had an idea of what I wanted to accomplish, many of the things were the work of others, derivatives of others' work or happenstance, and some of them could be classified as just plain luck," he said. Tansey's protestation aside, he was the *catalyst* present at each of York Container's moves forward, and the primary person who consistently looked for ways to help the company progress.

The *Madison Factor* at Work

In chemistry, a catalyst is something that does not force a reaction to happen, but speeds it up so that it happens now, rather than thousands of years from now. Leaders who play the role of the *Madison factor* or who act as the *Madison factor* are the catalysts for organizational change, bringing people along and keeping the momentum going until it is self-sustaining. Many of the strategic leaders interviewed pointed to their own *Madison factor* — people to whom the executive could turn to get the job done in critical areas.

Many organizations espouse change, but any transformational plan only has merit if it becomes self-sustaining. After the American Revolution, the government formed under the Articles of Confederation began to unravel without the unifying cause of the war. Washington, Madison, Hamilton, and others acted as the catalysts to create a new constitution and a new form of government. They convinced others of the importance of building a strong union, maintaining the gains of the Revolution, and establishing the new nation upon republican lines. But they did not stop there. Many of the key players of the Revolutionary Generation performed the *Madison factor* function, tirelessly carrying out the plan in the new Constitution. They went into every branch of local, state, and national government, working to translate the plan into action. They disagreed on tactics and policies and struggled with one another from the beginning. However, they all believed they were creating "a more perfect union" and were willing to continue to devote themselves to making their version of the plan a reality.

Today's successful strategic leaders follow their example and devote themselves to turning vision into reality, executing their plans, energizing their employees, and continuously improving their processes to sustain ever-improving results.

But how do these leaders, the framers and contemporaries, manage to bring along a large number of people, especially when the journey is perilous, painful, and unpredictable? How do they manage the realities and messiness of human nature?

Article VII

Nurturing Human Nature

"But what is government itself, but the greatest of all reflections on human nature? If men were angels, no government would be necessary."
— James Madison[1]

"All the passions then we see, of avarice, ambition, interest...Give all power to the many, they will oppress the few. Give all power to the few, they will oppress the many."
— Alexander Hamilton[2]

"There are two passions which have a powerful influence on the affairs of men. These are ambition and avarice; the love of power and the love of money."
— Benjamin Franklin[3]

The framers were astute observers of human nature; they tried to take it into account in every aspect of their planning. They had a clear-eyed understanding of individual and organizational psychology long before such terms were coined. Despite their admiration of the Enlightenment philosophers, they knew we humans are driven by our emotions, or what they called our "passions." The framers knew they needed systems to check those passions. They were more often on target than not, although they failed to see the rise of political parties, which skewed many of their plans.

Today's best leaders also are realistic about human nature. In addition to dealing with the darker side, strategic leaders engage people in positive ways so their "passions" mesh with the goals of the organization. Modern leaders know it takes an engaged workforce to implement their plans. The continuing breakthrough research of the Gallup organization confirms the power of this engagement.[4] Scott Adams' *Dilbert* cartoons entertain precisely because people recognize the counterparts in their organizations of the "pointy-haired boss" and "evil HR director" who are oblivious to human psychology.

George Washington was well acquainted with human nature, especially his own. According to many biographies, at an early age he began to tame and shape his human nature.[5] His monumental temper, usually kept under wraps, tripped him up more than once when he let it rip. As committed to republican ideals as he was, and as much as he wanted to believe that a positive human nature would triumph, his experience taught him otherwise. When farmers protesting foreclosures on their properties stormed the debtors' courts and sheriffs auctions during Shays' Rebellion, he wrote,

> 'We have probably had too good an opinion of human nature in forming our confederation...Experience has taught us that men will not adopt and carry into execution measures the best calculated for their own good, without the intervention of a coercive power'... [H]aving experienced personal betrayal and political chicanery at all levels of government, Washington knew first hand the levers of power and the petty intrigues that attended their use.
>
> As president, he harbored none of the modern reformer's illusions about human perfectibility.[6]

Successful modern leaders are not cynics; they are realistic about human behavior in all its negative and positive forms. They do not expect humans to be "angels."

Reason Tells Us We Are But Men

The political philosophy espoused by most of the framers rested on the understanding that humans would oppress one another when left to themselves. Jefferson reiterated this view in the Declaration of Independence: "That to secure these Rights, [Life, Liberty and the Pursuit of Happiness] Governments are instituted among Men...that whenever any Form of Government becomes destructive of these Ends, it is the Right of the People to alter or to abolish it." The framers constantly discussed the need to have a separation of powers in the executive, legislative, and judicial branches, each checking the power of the other.

During their debates, no issue, not even slavery, threatened to wreck the Constitutional Convention more than the question of allotting representation in the new legislature.[7] The delegates agreed generally on a bicameral system in which each house had different powers to act as checks on one another. In fact, most states already had such a system. Yet as they tried to determine how representation would be decided for each house, a chasm opened.

Put yourself in that oppressively hot and airless room again, overdressed and under-hydrated, as June wore on into July of 1787. Forget the image of men dispassionately discussing the issue of representation with courteous gentility; if you want a flavor of their debating style, watch the Prime Minister's "Question Time" in the British House of Commons on C-SPAN or the BBC. Following on the heels of the obligatory "Right Honorable Gentleman" form of address are barbs, thinly veiled attacks, devastating verbal assaults, and rude sounds of derision. The exchanges are probably closer to the tone of the Constitutional framers' exchanges as they wrangled over how to accommodate both large and small states. This is the messy process of coming to a decision.

Emotions are running high. Day after day, they circle and diverge and go back over the same issue. Tempers fray. A particularly bad day was June 30, a sultry Saturday. Delegates have dug in their heels. The small states fear they will be overpowered by the larger ones if representation is proportional to population. The large states fear the tyranny of the minority if all states have equal representation, as in the Confederation Congress.

> Feelings on both sides were so strong that a lot of the delegates were willing to sink the Convention rather than give in. Among them was Gunning Bedford, a fat, tempestuous delegate from Delaware...'He is a bold and nervous (agitated) speaker, and has a very commanding and striking manner; — but he is warm and impetuous in his temper, and precipitate in his judgment.'[8]

Bedford drags his bulk out of his chair and addresses the assembly, his temper rising as he accuses specific states of evil intent, fixing them one by one with his myopic stare. His intent is to offend and to voice what many from the small states were thinking.

> [States] act from interested, and many from ambitious motives. Look at the votes...it will be found that their numbers, wealth and local views, have actuated their determinations; and that the larger states proceed as if our eyes were already perfectly blinded. Impartiality, with them is already out of the question...They endeavor to amuse us with the purity of their principles and the rectitude of their intentions...Pretences to support ambition are never wanting...[The three largest states which] form nearly a majority of the people in America, [claim] they never will hurt or injure the lesser states. *I do not, gentlemen, trust you.* If you possess the power, the abuse of it could not be checked; and what then would prevent you from exercising it to our destruction?

> ...The small states never can agree to the Virginia plan...it is said that it is not expected that the state governments will approve the proposed system, and that this house must directly carry it to THE PEOPLE for their approbation! Is it come to this, then, that *the sword* must decide this controversy, and that the horrors of war must be added to the rest of our misfortunes?
>
> ...Will you crush the smaller states, or must they be left unmolested? Sooner than be ruined, there are foreign powers who will take us by the hand.[9]

Rufus King, a delegate from Massachusetts, cannot leave the threat of civil war and foreign intervention unchallenged. He confronts Bedford for his "intemperance" and "vehemence." "They had reached a hopeless impasse, and adjourned...Once again, fortuitously, just when tempers were at their hottest, a Sunday intervened."[10]

Tempers can run just as hot on modern teams. Taking a break lets people cool down. Trying to push an angry group to consensus is basically impossible, because emotions hold sway.

When the delegates reconvene on Monday, July 2, the debate on representation continues. Gouverneur Morris advocates a Senate with members elected for life and drawn from the financial and social elite. Otherwise, he predicts,

> The Rich will strive to establish their dominion & enslave the rest. They always did. They always will... So it will be among us.
>
> Reason tells us we are but men: and we are not to expect any particular interference of Heaven in our favor.[11]

The final compromise, with all states represented equally in the Senate and by population in the House, came on July 16.[12] The vehemence of the arguments and views almost all delegates expressed were based on their experience with human nature and their analysis of how people behaved throughout history. The sometimes frustratingly slow pace at which the U.S. government works reflects the framers' attempt to rein in our most negative tendencies and darkest natures through numerous checks and balances.

Creating cumbersome bureaucracies is *not* the lesson today's organizational leaders should take from this aspect of the Convention, dubbed the "Great Compromise." Modern leaders *should* examine human nature and psychology. How do people actually behave? How are people really motivated? To what extent will fear lead people to resist any change, no matter how positively communicated?

Initiatives are usually announced by leaders, often with great fanfare. When leaders simply assume employees will automatically embrace the change, they are *hoping* human nature will miraculously change. Leaders with a practical understanding of psychology act more like CEOs Howard Putnam of Southwest or Greg Swienton of Ryder System. These leaders talk to people one-on-one and in small groups. They listen to people. They bring people along, reinforcing the message at every opportunity. They understand most people won't change quickly. They work with human nature, not against it.

Teamwork is Not a Love-In

Every group experiences some rough spots when tempers flare and little work gets done. Successful leaders help the group learn to get beyond this inevitable friction and jell into a team. Dr. Bruce Tuckman's Stages of Team Development[13] describes predictable group behavior over time. After the awkwardness of the Forming stage, most groups enter a Storming period, as individuals begin to have a stake in the outcome and want their point of view to prevail. This stage is often characterized by overt conflict, secret agendas, challenges to the leader's authority, clique formation, and general lack of coherence or results.

The debates over representation and slavery in the Convention illustrate the Storming stage at its worst. Modern teams in the throes of such battles are generally incapable of making good, successful decisions, much less acting on them.

The leader's job is to help the team channel these "passions" and competing interests into a creative dialogue. By focusing on specific goals, the leader moves into the more productive Norming stage, when people are engaged, working more cooperatively, and taking on more responsibility for team success. Some teams even reach the Performing stage, when everyone fully commits, takes leadership responsibility, and actively supports team members.

Some leaders readily take on the task of creating these high-performing teams. Luda Kopeikina is such a leader. She was a vice president at GE, working with Jack Welch, and the CEO of two companies. Noventra, her current entrepreneurial venture, is focused on finding and developing new technologies which will positively impact the community at large.

Kopeikina built successful teams in every job she's held. She makes sure everyone expresses their ideas and challenges them to stay focused on ideas that reflect the mission. At Noventra, that focus is always, "will this have significant impact and value for the world at large?"

Part of building a successful team requires moving people into the "clarity state." She researched and documented this process and taught it to a variety of executives.[14]

> The key to reaching mastery in decision-making is the ability to focus your physical, mental, and emotional resources on an issue like a laser beam. Such focus enables you to reach decision clarity faster and easier...**Clarity** is a feeling of certainty and of internal alignment with the solution. **The objective of a decision-making process is to reach clarity. A**

right decision is one when the decision maker is emotionally and mentally congruent with it...Many business executives stressed the following three characteristics of reaching a clear decision...Positive Charge...Commitment to a Vision...Minimal Post-Decision Doubts...You cannot lead without reaching clarity first!

...Clarity state is the state of being

- Physically relaxed
- Emotionally positive, happy, released from fear and anxiety
- Charged with power, success, self-confidence, and energy
- Totally in the present
- Mentally focused on the task at hand. [To reach the clarity state] prepare, relax your body, calm your mind, clear your mind, charge up.

Kopeikina employs her clarity-state methodology with her own team and trained all of her managers to use it. "The creativity when you're in the clarity state is great," she reports. Because one of the hallmarks of the methodology is encouraging conflict, "I encourage managers to set up the situation so there is conflict. Otherwise, you might be prone to goody-goody types of impact. When there are conflicting opinions, you might put creative ideas on the table and you might be getting something worthwhile."

Reaching the clarity state cannot be over-emphasized. As described in Article V, Madison made himself ill in trying to solve the issue of slavery. He never reached clarity; he was never "emotionally and mentally congruent" with his decisions. Without clarity, even Madison's vast intelligence and problem-solving skills were not sufficient to craft a creative and practical solution he could execute. Washington was able to reach clarity after a lifetime of evolving his views on race. He reached clarity at the end of his life, and freed his slaves in his will.

Kopeikina knows everyone's ideas must be heard and all ideas seriously considered to make messy, creative conflict work.

> I try to be upfront with everyone, 'Hey, we might not be able to implement all of these ideas. Your idea might be good, but we want to use another one.' People understand that and are contributing ideas that are good for the overall company and benefit our growth. People do give and take.
>
> It's only when you let things go too long and people get too attached to an idea where they start to have a vested interest when problems arise. Sometimes, I even bring in outside judges and let people present their ideas while I stay silent. Then they accept the decision that one idea was much better.

When Kopeikina finds a team member who is overwhelmed with ideas, she encourages the person to relax and just observe. Idea generation will eventually subside; then the person can move back into the discussion on solutions.

Successful strategic leaders like Kopeikina understand these key factors of human nature:

- People are creative, and when challenged to be creative, they will oblige;
- Setting clear objectives and staying focused on them helps channel creativity into productive paths;
- Providing space for people to move in and out of the fray as they need to for their own comfort reduces the stress that inhibits creativity; and,

- People are more likely to implement solutions they have been involved in producing, even when the final idea is not one hundred percent their own.

The Constitutional framers understood human behavior because of years of observation and deep thinking. The most successful framers were able to apply their knowledge in everyday situations.

For example, Madison, although uncomfortable in large groups, was affable and witty in small gatherings. He put people at ease; he influenced them by listening to and understanding their concerns, as well as by proposing livable compromises. In any debate, his meticulous preparation allowed him to craft persuasive arguments that resonated with people's emotions without being emotional.

Not all leaders are as skilled and knowledgeable as Madison and Kopeikina. Some modern leaders lack a basic knowledge of human psychology or group dynamics. They are stymied by acrimonious discussions and frustrated by lack of cooperation and progress. They mistakenly focus on "team building" and "bonding", hoping an outside facilitator will accomplish what they cannot.

For example, a social services provider experienced major difficulties and devastating conflicts among the staff for more than a year. The executive director decided the supervisory staff should spend a half day in a ropes course, believing the team would "bond" and do a better job because of the shared experience.[15] Many of the sullen and dispirited employees of the agency straggled to the site the morning of the event, dressed and shod for dancing and clubbing, not climbing up a wall. Angry and resentful, they weren't about to bond or make a dent in their deep-seated problems.

In another situation, an industry association's board chair insisted the board members and staff should have some "team-building games" as part of their strategic planning session. The participants managed to cover their negative thoughts about such activities a little better than the social services group; they *accidentally* lost the game props.

Team coherence *is* important among executives, managers, and employees who must work cooperatively to reach their stated goals. Yet teamwork does not come from these artificial activities. In fact, recent research by the Hay Group, cited in the Postscript, found these activities often lack long-term effectiveness. On the other hand, the leadership team from Southwest Airlines got together for a Texas barbecue. It helped them loosen up and become more creative because it was a natural, casual event, not an orchestrated workshop with planned exercises and defined outcomes.

The framers at the convention socialized, attended entertainment and educational events, engaged in sports, and pursued other leisure activities together. They were folks who knew how to have a good time, and most were adept at social discourse. When they were entombed in the assembly room or the committee rooms, however, they had to develop working alliances and find practical compromises — regardless of whether they liked one another. Their natural socializing eased the way, as it does with modern teams, but does not guarantee success, cooperation, or great decision-making.

Team Doesn't Have an "I" but it Has a ME!

Many members of the Revolutionary Generation shared strong bonds, forged in their work to create a new country and government. As seen from the extended and sometimes rancorous debates, however, they did *not* all agree with one another. It is also clear that some delegates did not like one another. A few excerpts from their letters and diaries tell the story:

> I mix with company without enjoying it...To be very fashionable we must be very trifling and make and receive a thousand professions which everybody knows there is not truth in. – Oliver Ellsworth to his wife[16]

"My hopes of returning by the time expected are a little clouded by reason of there being certain creatures in this world that are more pleased with their speeches than they can (prevail) upon any body else to be."
—William Livingston to his son-in-law, John Jay[17]

"We move slowly in our business...impeded at every step by jealousies and jarring interests."
—William Richardson Davie to Governor Caswell of North Carolina[18]

"You may have been taught said [George Mason] to respect the Characters of the Members of the late Convention. You may have supposed that they were an assemblage of great Men. There is nothing less true...there were Knaves and Fools...[and] Office Hunters not a few."
—Hugh Williamson reporting George Mason's view of his fellow delegates to John Blount.[19]

This latter is in stark contrast to the assessment of Thomas Jefferson that the Convention was "an assembly of demi-gods" and Benjamin Franklin's description that they were "une assemblée des notables[,] A convention composed of some of the principal people from the several States of our confederation."[20]

Create Constancy of Purpose

If you cannot create teamwork artificially, then how is it done? First, a unifying vision and mission build a culture, as discussed in Articles II and III. Dr. W. Edwards Deming's first admonition in his classic fourteen points for management is, "create constancy of purpose."[21] Gibraltar Private Bank and Trust offers an exemplary team-building model through its joint performance goals.

Teamwork at Gibraltar evolved. At first, the prognosis was

not great. Like all companies, there were natural tensions between departments charged with selling products and those working to fulfill those sales. The mortgage banking group had very robust goals for revenues and profits. The sales group complained the group which processed applications and prepared closing documents was not turning them around quickly enough. In turn, the processing group complained the sales group did not provide all the needed information and set unrealistic turnaround times.

These same conflicts were observed in the case of another bank we'll identify as ABC Bank, where an impasse developed between the commercial loan officers and the loan processors. Both groups had unrealistic expectations; both lobbed verbal grenades. The loan processors *had* streamlined their processes and shaved turnaround time for loans significantly. Despite this, the processors could not get any traction with the loan officers to get complete, correct loan application information.

Both the loan officers and the loan processors were psychologically framed in their approaches to solving the problem. The loan processors frame was, "loan officers should know certain information. They don't provide it because they don't care." The loan officers' frame was, "paperwork is beneath us. It's the purview of the clerks." They always referred to loan processors derisively as "clerks."

The loan officers never received training in the details of compiling information for complex business loans. Their monetary incentive was to produce more loans, not provide complete information to the processors. Their angry state kept them spinning in place. The loan officers even refused to meet with the loan processors.

The CEO of ABC Bank was blind to the way the incentive system, class antagonisms, and blame environment framed the worst of their human nature. The CEO saw the situation as a "you can't get good help around here" problem. Nothing changed.

In dramatic contrast, Gibraltar Private Bank created an innovative solution and performance improved dramatically. The mortgage sales and mortgage processing groups set joint goals and targets. One group could not be successful without the cooperation of the other. They met together, analyzed their workflow and bottlenecks, and developed more efficient processes. Gibraltar's CEO and CFO praised the joint work, rewarded it, and encouraged others to take the same initiative. There was no singing *Kumbaya* around the campfire, no false comradeship, and no artificial appeals to bond — just joint work that created success for each department.

Steve Hayworth, CEO, Gibraltar Bank: One of the things I enjoy so much about our company is that we have a lot of spirited, opinionated people who are very good at what they do. They're very passionate about what they do and they're not bashful. What helped us, as a group, was going through the strategic-planning process together and avoiding the temptation to say, 'I'm right, you're wrong.' At the end of the day, we came out with our marching orders for all of us. The litmus test is, 'Is it consistent with our goals?' It created an esprit de corps where it wasn't departmental or siloed. That helped us move the strategic-planning process along so everybody in the organization was engaged.

What we're finding out now is how every department is interdependent with the others. Marketing is spending more and more time with the human resources function and deposit operations. That has been a specific outcome of these departmental plans going through the human resources function. That was a critical component to getting strategic planning throughout the whole organization, to get the teamwork and team building we needed to make it happen. We're still in the early phases of it, but we're seeing a lot more interaction.

We've created another special group with a specific plan, touching everyone in this bank.

Tony Caron, CFO, Gibraltar: That's a group that was actually envisioned and created as a result of the strategic planning. It probably speaks more to the Gibraltar experience than any other. It was a product of the strategic-planning process because the resources and competencies necessary to get us to the next level organizationally were not going to come from one department.

Teamwork at Gibraltar grew organically from people setting joint goals and working to meet those joint goals — just as it did at the Constitutional Convention. "Teamwork," as an organizational value, comes up over and over, from giant corporations to small nonprofits. In successful organizations such as Gibraltar, teams become teams through shared goals and working to meet those goals.

Setting joint departmental goals does not guarantee success, however. For example, in another company, several departments set excellent joint goals. When their leader did not hold people accountable, the plan faltered and the outcomes never fully materialized. No one saw the failures as a problem, although there were serious repercussions.

Teamwork evolves when people are *held responsible for mutual success* and work together to achieve it.

An Unlikely Team

To make the strategy of joint goal-setting succeed requires strong commitment from each partner but they don't *have* to be best buddies. Look at James Madison and Alexander Hamilton. It's hard to find two more different Constitutional framers. Both had towering intellects, but there the similarities end. Madison was quiet, usually calm, a born facilitator, subdued in dress and manner and a devoted, faithful husband. Hamilton was flamboyant, outspoken and often rash, something of a dandy, and had well-known extramarital affairs. During the Revolution, Hamilton served as Washington's aide, but finally fulfilled his dreams of glory as an artillery officer. He led a charge on General Charles Cornwallis' entrenched forces at Yorktown, helping defeat the British. Meanwhile, Madison served in the Continental Congress and the Virginia legislature, mastering legislative politics. (As President during the War of 1812 with Britain, he did take to the field and showed great valor.)[22]

These unlikely teammates worked together to engineer the Constitutional Convention, and afterward, they collaborated to write most of the essays in *The Federalist*. They produced the work in the white heat of creativity over a few months. They seldom had a chance to edit or comment on one another's work before it was published, but their thinking was completely aligned.[23] Although scholars can discuss differences, these remarkable essays speak with one voice. This team effort is acclaimed as one of the most important political works in American history.

In the early days of the Republic, Hamilton, as Secretary of the Treasury, was charged with creating a financial plan for the government. Just as Madison was an expert on governance and constitutions, Hamilton studied money, finance, and debt, and was arguably the most knowledgeable expert in the U.S. on these subjects.

When he brought his complex plan to the Congress, there was massive resistance, and one of the critics was Madison. Among other things, Hamilton called for the federal government to "assume" — code for take full responsibility for — the war debts of the states, consolidate them, issue bonds to fund the debt, and establish a national bank. The thorny issues, subsumed under this proposal for "assumption," created a political tsunami that threatened the fragile new government. Something had to give.

Supposedly, Jefferson hosted a dinner party where Hamilton and Madison struck a deal.[24] Whatever actually happened — the principals were always a little coy when discussing it later in life — Hamilton and Madison once again collaborated as a team, despite their growing personal and political distance. Madison twisted enough arms to assure the assumption plan passed the House of Representatives with a wide enough margin so he could save face with his own constituency and vote against it.

A Team of Best Buds

Jefferson and Madison, in contrast, were a team of actual best friends. Not long after the assumption battle, they plotted to destroy Hamilton politically. They engaged in some of the most deceitful acts imaginable, displaying behaviors we usually associate with the worst of corporate or public politics, backbiting, and character assassination. As the Hamilton-Madison team unraveled, each man formed a new team and infant political parties emerged.

For example, during Washington's second term as President, renewed war between France and Britain threatened to draw America into the conflict. Washington wanted to maintain a policy of strict neutrality, which was not acceptable to either combatant. Edmund Charles Genêt, also known as Citizen Genêt, the representative from revolutionary France, was stirring the pot of discontent in the U.S., trying to pressure Washington to support France. Quarrelsome cabinet members Hamilton and Jefferson were at odds over what to do, with Hamilton supporting Britain and Jefferson, France. During one of the ensuing battles between the emerging parties of Jefferson and Hamilton,

> A renewed journalistic war broke out as Hamilton defended Washington's proclamation [of neutrality in the war between France and England] in print and

Madison raised the specter of executive domination. So powerfully did Hamilton contend for the president's foreign policy franchise that he provoked a desperate appeal from Jefferson to his political consort. "For God's sake, my dear sir," he told Madison, "take up your pen, select the most striking heresies, and cut him to pieces in the face of the public. There is nobody who can and will enter the lists with him."[25]

As the internecine battles continued, Jefferson left Washington's cabinet. When some of Madison's underhanded attacks were exposed, his relationship with Washington, solidified during the Constitutional Convention, ruptured completely. Washington could no longer rely on his "Madison Factor."

Human nature doesn't always allow teamwork. Even Washington could not overcome the juggernaut of the warring factions in his cabinet. By that time, the individuals no longer shared the same unifying interpretation of the country's vision and mission. They were committed to building very different cultures. Washington, unlike Hayworth at Gibraltar Bank, had no way to reward joint achievements. Even Washington's force of character could not heal the widening split.

Human Nature is Not All Gloom and Doom

Successful leaders can have no illusions about the negative aspects of human nature. On the other hand, they cannot ignore the potential of the positive aspects. Ben Baldanza, CEO of Spirit Airlines, exemplifies modern leaders who understand what it takes to engage employees fully and build high-functioning teams by using motivational psychology. He describes one of the main pillars of his strategy for growing the airline.

I want Spirit to be the best place to work in the

airline business. Fundamentally, airlines are service industries run by people, for people, and about people. Having employees enjoy coming to work isn't just a good thing to do as human beings; it's good business. Employees who love their jobs are going to smile more at customers. They're going to get less rattled in pressure situations. They're naturally going to want to treat customers better.

Treating our employees well, hiring the right people for the jobs, providing good feedback mechanisms, talking to employees, providing good incentive plans, and rewarding appropriate behaviors, are all part of that dynamic.

Clarence Otis, CEO of Darden Restaurants, applies his knowledge of human psychology not only with employees, but also with customers of his casual dining restaurants — Bahama Breeze, The Capital Grille, Longhorn Steakhouse, Olive Garden, Red Lobster, Seasons 52, and Smokey Bones Barbeque and Grill. When he surveys customers, they say they want healthier choices in their casual dining. But according to Otis,

> There's a disconnect between consumer attitudes and consumer behavior. The biggest diversion is around eating healthy. People don't really order the healthier things on the menu. But at the same time, people say they would like to eat healthier. So we work hard to make the recipes that we develop as healthy as they can be, without compromising flavor and appeal.

When Darden launched their Seasons 52 restaurants, Otis drew on his understanding of this paradox of human nature. "When you communicate healthy to people, they think they have to compromise on taste. So the way we've positioned these restaurants is around fresh, seasonal food that is a culinary treat and tastes good." When people read the menu, they discover the dishes are healthier, under 475 calories, and prepared with minimal fats and frying.

Successful leaders learn about human nature by a combination of intuitive knowledge, observation, experience, and formal study. Ed Novak, a former senior vice president at Bank of America, was asked to speak at a conference on software quality because he headed up several large technology initiatives for the bank. He brought along his lead project manager and shared the stage with her. This was highly unusual for an executive keynote speaker. When asked about it, he replied, "I didn't know any better. I thought everybody teamed up." Novak expanded on his team approach:

> My job is to deal with clients and work with our technology partners. We deliver systems that give our client-touching folks information about where they're being successful and where they need improvement. I'm a banker. I don't know the technology side. I knew my weaknesses and knew I needed somebody who understood technology and could get our vision built. My value would be understanding our business.
>
> I saw, from day one, that it was a partnership. We would partner to be successful. That's worked for the last eight years. It wasn't any stroke of brilliance. This was the only way I could think of going about it to be successful.

Novak's modesty aside, his way of partnering for success has become a best practice within the bank and is widely emulated. And Novak knows something else critical about human nature — people want a challenge. People want to succeed. Novak has been successful in harnessing that positive energy.

One of the key pieces is a shared understanding of

the importance of what we're doing. I look for people who take an interest in what we're trying to do. What distinguishes that person is a willingness to take ownership of the outcome. People push themselves and others, not in a 'crack the whip' kind of way, but in helping one another see the importance.

I was on a conference call one night and one of the people said to another, 'You've got to rerun the data.' The other person said, 'It's after five o'clock. It won't happen.' Then the first person said, 'Wait a minute, folks. We're at a point where time is critical for our results.' The other person said, 'I hear you. We'll get it done.' Our team is willing to push for the good of the cause, and [they] help one another see the benefit of what needs to be done.

Successful leaders like Novak not only set the bar high, but also understand another aspect of human nature. They expect, get, and reward exceptional behavior, and they lead by example. As Novak expresses it, "I don't ask them to do anything I haven't done or still am willing to do for us to be a success."

Tapping Into the Reality of Human Nature

Stephanie Sonnabend, President and co-CEO of Sonesta International Hotels Corporation, serves with her cousin, Peter Sonnabend, who is co-CEO and vice president. She faces the twin challenges of competing in an environment dominated by large hotel chains and one where she must keep the brand fresh and vibrant. She understands the key ingredient for her success is the people who work in every hotel, especially those who must translate lofty corporate ideals into day-to-day interaction with guests.

Sonesta owns hotels around the globe. Each is marketed

as a unique destination reflecting the culture and ambiance of its location. Stephanie Sonnabend was a liberal arts major at Harvard and got an MBA from the Massachusetts Institute of Technology's Sloan School of Management. She brings both types of education to her thinking on the job. "I think quite broadly and in possibilities. I think about how to differentiate us. Then I apply the more technical business thinking about where we are in our product cycle. How do we continue to keep the company's brand fresh? How do we communicate that vision throughout the company?"

She said the secret has been "enrolling other people and getting them on the same page." She engages employees at every level of the organization, focusing on evolving the corporate culture based on core values. Yet she is the first to admit that at each hotel property, many people are more concerned with what's happening at that local level.

She has found that "involving people in conversations bigger than themselves" helps get staff in far-flung locations to understand and implement the company's core values.

> Sonesta's people are very loyal and stay with us for a long time. That means they may not be exposed to thinking beyond what they know. So I work to get them that exposure. For example, we get accounting people to attend marketing meetings and broaden their exposure. We encourage many people to attend conferences where they're exposed to the thinking in other companies. As we bring in new people… who have a different perspective, we applaud that and say, 'Okay. What can we learn from these new people?'

To keep ideas coming from all parts of the organization, to build the necessary engagement, Sonnabend instituted a meeting at each hotel property to brainstorm ideas before developing the company's marketing and budget plans.

We get people in small groups and allow everyone to participate. I attended a few of them, but I find that it's better if I don't, so people are freer to come up with more ideas. I know people do listen to me, and I drive a lot of the strategy. The real value is in including people in the process, even when we can't implement all of the ideas.

We do the same at the corporate level and bring in the field people to help develop the corporate strategy. Each property implements the strategies with its own specific flavor. It's important that the hotels create their own plans and strategies.

Local employees might not care about the corporate financial strategy, but we help them understand our values and how to incorporate them in their day-to-day work. We are sensitive to their priorities.

She also empowered general managers at each property to be "kings of their own castles." Although she reviews their plans, she leaves it up to them to make and execute the plans, to be responsible for results and solutions. She also challenges them and encourages them to think in fresh ways. She coaches them, but makes sure she has delegated the authority they need along with the responsibility so they are both empowered and engaged, and can handle the details. "I build consensus and take a lot of input before I make a decision where I need to have buy in and enroll people in implementing that decision."

Nurturing Nature

Today's leaders have access to more data about human nature than the framers did. In the end, they don't necessarily need all the data, if, like the most successful framers, they are accurate and perceptive observers of the humans around them. Great leaders know both our dark side and how to bring out the best by challenging us to follow their example, to reach inside ourselves and unleash our talents.

George Washington became the iconic leader he was for his contemporaries not because he was the best general or most articulate speaker, but because he had the ability to spot and develop talent. He could convince individuals or groups they could make a difference. He seldom failed to lead by example, and instinctively knew when to allow decision-making to proceed without interfering and inadvertently squelching debate.

Today's successful leaders, whether realizing it or not, follow Washington's example. They tap into the synergy of the group for the best ideas, and encourage debate and discussion to tease out the best ideas. They engage employees through participation in planning what they will implement. They give people both the responsibility and authority to get results. They nurture the best parts of our human nature.

Yet even the much-admired Constitutional framers did not get everything right the first time. How do successful leaders make sure the organization is reinvented periodically and is always evolving? How do leaders create a "more perfect" organization, just as the framers wanted to create a "more perfect union?"

Amendments

Failure to Improve Is Not an Option

The Congress, whenever two thirds of both Houses shall deem it necessary, shall propose Amendments to the Constitution...which...shall be valid to all Intents and Purposes, as Part of this Constitution, when ratified by the Legislatures of three fourths of the Several States...
— *Article V, US Constitution*

When Apollo 13 Flight Director, Gene Kranz,[1] uttered those now-classic words, "Failure is not an option!", he might have been speaking for the U.S. founders and framers and modern organizational leaders. Through the darkest days of the American Revolution, the military leaders in the field and the political leaders in the constantly-relocating Continental Congress knew there was no going back, no compromising, and no giving up. They could expect no mercy from the British. The ones we still honor were absolutely serious when they pledged "our Lives, our Fortunes, and our sacred Honor." Still later, as the conspirators brought about the Constitutional Convention, and then fought through the ratification process, they believed fiercely that *failure was not an option.*

The contemporary leaders in this book also took that motto as their own. Yet dealing with major crises is not the only threat organizations face. Failure to improve in a highly competitive environment is also an important threat. At the end of the Convention, Benjamin Franklin pointed out that the Constitution was probably the best they could do under the circumstances. The delegates obviously agreed, and added an amendment process in Article V that did not require one hundred percent agreement among the states, as had the doomed Articles of Confederation.

The way to stave off failure is to improve continuously. This strategy is a fundamental one for historical and contemporary leaders.

The Bill of Rights – A Classic Continuous Improvement Project

Before the Constitutional Convention delegates began signing their names on the new document, strong opposition to the new Constitution was fomenting. Patrick Henry of Virginia, Governor George Clinton of New York, and other entrenched, powerful state politicians, mounted a vigorous fight to prevent ratification. They were not about to give up the sovereignty of the states to a national government. Other opponents, however, believed strongly that the document was hopelessly flawed without an enumeration of individual rights such as appeared in many state constitutions at the time. In the end, only three of the delegates still at the Convention refused to sign: Governor Edmund Randolph, who had presented the original Virginia Plan, George Mason, another Virginia delegate, and Elbridge Gerry[2] from Massachusetts.

The issue of the enumeration of rights had come up several times in the convention; each time, James Madison and others had opposed it. In *Federalist* 58, Alexander Hamilton, writing as Publius, argued forcefully against a Bill of Rights.[3] He laid out three strong reasons: enumerating individual rights could actually limit them if the list were not one hundred percent inclusive; the Constitution gave no power to the national government to take away individual rights; and the Constitution protected certain critical rights, specifically those guaranteeing individual liberties and republican principles.

> Here, in strictness, the people surrender nothing; and as they retain every thing they have no need of

particular reservations. 'We, the People of the United States, to secure the blessings of liberty to ourselves and our posterity, do ordain and establish this Constitution for the United States of America.' Here is a better recognition of popular rights, than volumes of those aphorisms which make the principal figure in several of our State bills of rights...

But a minute detail of particular rights is certainly far less applicable to a Constitution like that under consideration, which is merely intended to regulate the general political interests of the nation...I go further, and affirm that bills of rights...are not only unnecessary in the proposed Constitution, but would even be dangerous. They would contain various exceptions to powers not granted; and...would afford a colorable pretext to claim more than were granted. For why declare that things shall not be done which there is no power to do?[4]

Although Madison and his compatriots won the argument at the Convention, the anti-Federalists clearly were not going to let the issue die. In fact, Madison was not going to be able to garner the support he needed to get ratification in Virginia without such a bill. Several other key states were heading down the same non-ratification path. Even more alarming were calls for a *new* convention or for regular conventions to reconsider the entire Constitution. Knowing how difficult it had been to get the agreements and compromises they *had* achieved, Madison knew another convention would lead to disaster and the break up of the fragile union.

So, Madison agreed to activate the Amendment clause for continuous improvement in the Constitution.[5] He agreed to carry amendments into the newly-formed Congress and fight for their inclusion during the amending process. He collected all the proposed amendments from the various states and consolidated them into twelve. Ten of them passed and became the Bill of Rights, the first ten amendments to the Constitution ratified by the states in 1791.

The framers created the crucial amendment process because they understood that, no matter how good they thought their product was, they were fallible human beings. They knew some of their compromises were weak links and might break. There must be a way both to fix mistakes and allow for innovations they could not even imagine.

Only twenty-seven amendments have been ratified after over two hundred years, a measure of the quality of the original document. Amendments abolishing slavery, expanding suffrage to all adult citizens, popularly electing senators, and strengthening presidential succession in case of death, corrected major defects in the original.

Contemporary Continuous Improvement Spiral

Continuous improvement keeps the Constitution alive and evolving as society changes. The ongoing development of the modern continuous improvement philosophy keeps companies alive and evolving as the environment changes.

When Drs. W. Edwards Deming, Joseph M. Juran, Kaoru Ishikawa, and others pioneered the modern quality movement in the wake of World War II, they wanted to unleash the potential of all employees to be engaged in improving their work processes. These management gurus[6] understood improvement begins at the top. Executives must adopt a philosophy focused on guaranteeing customers receive the product or service expected.

The journey of continuous improvement can be viewed as climbing a spiral staircase. With each turn, you arrive where you were, yet at a slightly higher level. The quality movement has continued to mature since its inception. Motorola, a continuous quality leader, building on the foundation of Deming, Juran, and Ishikawa, pioneered the next evolutionary stage, Six Sigma.[7] Jack Welch, when he was CEO at GE, picked up the approach and began proselytizing for its adoption throughout industry. The 1990s saw a revival of interest in this "new" approach, which continues to evolve and morph into new incarnations of the quality philosophy such as "lean manufacturing" and a plethora of innovative applications.[8]

In a few years, there will be another "new" approach based on the same fundamental quality principles, likely with a deeper and more sophisticated understanding of them at the next higher level of the spiral staircase. In Dr. Deming's formulation, people will have gained a more profound knowledge of their processes and can act on that understanding.

Improving Results

In discussing continuous improvement, we are not trying to imply the activities of contemporary leaders are in the same league with the accomplishments of the Constitutional framers. We *are* pointing out the parallels in the philosophical approaches and processes they followed.

Some of the interviewed leaders have implemented formal improvement efforts, while others simply encourage employees to look for better ways to do their tasks. Each went about improvement in a different way, yet each one's results demonstrate the soundness of the quality principles and the variety of ways they can be applied to turn vision into reality.

Maintaining an attitude of continuous improvement came naturally to Evan Rees, the former president of CNL Bank. He brought that approach with him as he moved through a number of executive positions in several regional banks. "I try to get people on my team who are smarter than me, people I can learn from. I tried to learn from *my* bosses. One told me I internalized what he said and make it happen. I think through what they're doing and learn from it."

The other approach Rees has practiced is to learn from competitors. "Your competition is your best friend. Anytime you have good competitors, you learn. You can improve your products and services. You can be very consistent in your delivery to your customers." As Rees took new assignments during a period of dynamic shifts and growth in the regional banking industry, he racked up a string of successes, building effective sales forces and branch operations by continuously improving his own performance and that of his teams.

Transformation at Ryder System

When Greg Swienton took the wheel as CEO of Ryder System, the company was in need of improvements. He had degrees in marketing and finance, and had cycled through executive positions in telecommunications and transportation.

> I remember when I first took this job. I said to people, 'I feel like I've been preparing my whole life to get to this position.'
>
> One of the reasons I joined Ryder was to ensure that the company really could fulfill its potential. I think, as with many other organizations, this is one that has so many good things going for it. It had a good long history and a track record. It had a very good brand name. It had very dedicated, good people. But it hadn't always been consistent in its performance.

Swienton's first step in transforming the company was to set a clear direction through a vision that the company "will be recognized as a consistent performer, and an investment that the shareholders find to be exceptional. I think we've been making a lot of progress in that regard. We have a company where employees are really proud to work, and where customers seek the solutions we put in place."

As Swienton communicated relentlessly with his 27,000

employees worldwide, he also put formal improvement efforts in place. He intuitively grasped one of Dr. Deming's major principles, consistent performance. According to Swienton,

> We've taken out $230 million in costs over three to four years. That included margin improvement teams that worked on the way we did business, reviewing the processes in different segments of the business. It was very much a process-driven approach and serves as a template throughout the organization. I think you always have to renew that and keep after it. In our case, that was a major issue as part of our transformation early on.

Swienton integrated his improvement efforts into the strategic planning for the company, another key quality principle. After Swienton's leadership team decides on the strategic direction, they focus on "a half dozen areas where we're going to spend more time, as opposed to constantly having this great big universe of potential opportunity." Such focus is a key component of continuous improvement. Swienton believes the time he spent in the seminary as a young man taught him the importance of the discipline and focus he brings to his work.

As an ardent admirer of the founding fathers, Swienton's discussions are peppered with references to these men and what he learned from them. When the series *John Adams* ran on HBO,[9] he not only watched it, but he also spent time discussing each episode with people at work, digging out important object lessons. What he admired about Adams was his tenacity, discipline, and focus.

Conversely, Swienton sees Adams' lack of flexibility as a failing point. Adams often dug into a position and refused to change with circumstances. Swienton knows flexibility is another hallmark of continuous improvement. He and his team are prepared to make revisions when necessary.

No battle plan has ever been able to be implemented as intended the moment you hit the beach or engage the enemy. It's no different in business. You don't know what the economic environment might be, what world events might occur, what's happening with the customer base, or whether the industry is moving up or in decline.

You have to stay on top of that constantly and formally. We look at the feedback and say, 'We see storm clouds, or opportunities, or we need a new course direction.' We have informal conversations with people about their businesses and say, 'Give me a feel for what you see, as opposed to what I see in the numbers.' You can't manage by numbers alone. You have to manage by both the people and the reality of what they are coming across in their day-to-day activity.

You have that gut feel and the numbers to help you do the right thing. Hoping it might self-correct is impossible. It will never self-correct.

Swienton's view on self-correction illustrates another important aspect of continuous improvement: hoping is not a strategy. No matter how well intentioned and determined people are, a process has a measurable performance capability that does not change by itself. Only one way exists to get better results: change the process to change those results. The product is only as good as the process that produces it. Swienton and his team changed the mission-critical processes to accomplish the transformation of the company.

Within three days of becoming CEO, I had a meeting of all our vice presidents and officers. It was really the beginning of our commitment to fulfill our potential. We met for several days and talked about the huge changes we had to make. This was the genesis of our cost-reduction improvement efforts to make us competitive and transform the business. We all signed a parchment so we would have the physical act, a manifestation, of our commitment. I guess I borrowed that idea from the framers. It's been hanging on my wall since 2000.

Transforming Ryder System was not painless. Continuous improvement means change. Sometimes that change is tough and has a negative effect on employees, whether by losing a job or being reassigned involuntarily. Swienton, like other executives, pointed to decisions that impacted people as being the hardest.

I was sent here to improve things, and very often that means a change of processes or structures, and invariably people are going to be involved. You want to ensure that you preserve the greatest good possible for the largest number of people, but sometimes the numbers just don't work. So I say to managers, 'Remember, this is an impact to a human being, a person with a family. It's somebody's career. Let's make sure that, before we impact that person, we have done everything else to take out every other peripheral, unnecessary cost, even if it affects our own convenience.'

After Swienton stabilized the company and assured its long-term success, his focus shifted to building again. Too often, companies transform themselves only to quickly ossify again. He realized that it was time for the continuous part of "continuous improvement" to kick in.

We had been so focused on improving returns and costs that I had to make a really, really concentrated effort, starting with myself, to make sure everybody understood what was important now that we were stable. Cost-cutting was not an endgame. It was to build a platform for the future. I told people, 'We're going for long-term sustainable and profitable growth.' I had to reawaken the organization.

I know I shocked two of our managers when they came in with their 2004 budget and showed me what they were cutting. I said, 'Why are we doing that? It's time to grow.'

Like the framers with their amendment process, Swienton opted for continuous improvement as *the* strategy to deal with new challenges and remedy old ones. Under his leadership, Ryder has continued its transformation and growth in good times and bad.

Gradual Change at York Container Company

The principles of continuous improvement do not require a Fortune 500 rating. York Container Company is located in the bucolic rolling hills of York, Pennsylvania, where the roving Continental Congress took refuge from the British army during the Revolution.[10] A family-owned business established in the 1950s, York is typical of small and mid-sized manufacturing companies trying to succeed in a mature market.

Beginning in the late 1980s, the company tried a series of improvement efforts based on the work of various quality experts, including Dr. Deming. The company had some successes but could not sustain the momentum for a variety of reasons. Despite its good reputation and apparently expanding revenues, multiple analyses demonstrated performance on key financial indicators was either flat or declining. As Steve Tansey moved into the newly created COO position, he knew he must make major changes to respond effectively to the current challenges.

Like Greg Swienton, Tansey recognized he could not

improve everything at once. As he gained the trust of both employees and owners, he worked gradually to change one significant aspect of the company after another. He also knew he had to figure out ways to strengthen the leadership team even though he was not the top executive. Tansey started this process by elevating one of the salesmen to sales manager. In his new position, the sales manager reinvigorated the sales team to such an extent that, Tansey admits, he had to hold them back a little until the plant production processes caught up. "My sales guys were literally on a leash. There was opportunity galore and it drove them crazy because they saw what they could do. The flip side of that is that my plant couldn't keep up with it, even running three shifts."

With the sales force functioning well, Tansey turned his attention to the plant. In the past at York, the press of work always seemed to overwhelm the early enthusiasm for process improvement, so Tansey decided to take a less direct approach. He started working with one of the machine operators. He asked him to take responsibility for coming up with metrics that could help him manage his operations.

> The operator noticed that when we produced a particular type of carton, we get a lot of waste. He went through root cause analysis and started moving upstream in the process, and was able to demonstrate that the problem was in another machine that wasn't printing properly. We made a series of alterations to the problem machine until we got good, consistent performance.
>
> The really exciting thing is that as he was doing this work on one machine, the operator on the next machine started coming over and asking, 'What are you guys doing over here? What's going on?' So there's the beginning of interest on the part of more operators.

Tansey also followed one of the tenets of excellence

mentioned by several executives who had been influenced by Jim Collins' book, *Good To Great*.[11] He hired for talent. To paraphrase Collins' analogy of the bus, "Get the right people on the bus and then get them in the right seats." And that's exactly what Tansey has done. He brought in an individual who was an engineer. His first assignment was to revitalize customer service. He succeeded brilliantly because he focused on defining efficient and effective processes.

When customer service was working smoothly, Tansey moved the man into a position to implement a new software system. Once again, the man excelled and proved his ability to produce praiseworthy results. The new system made many people's lives easier. Tansey has now moved him into yet another challenging position, this time to transform production. The man is Tansey's *Madison factor*.

Without declaring yet another new quality initiative and inviting a cynical backlash from employees who have seen these programs come and go, Tansey quietly and steadily improved company operations. The results showed up on the bottom line with record-setting growth for the company.

Revitalizing Oakland Park

The City of Oakland Park, Florida represents another and very different example of continuous improvement. When John Stunson took over as city manager in 2001, he was forced to lay people off and make other tough decisions to alleviate a major financial crisis. "In going through that, I tried to build in some severance and let people know before everything went public. There's always fallout, and it takes time for the organization to recover." Yet Stunson was able to get the city back on track as described in Article II. After the initial crisis was under control, he began expanding the city's tax base, revitalizing much of its decaying infrastructure, and engaging community activists to support the progress while bringing in key staff to assure that the improvements could be sustained.

With almost 43,000 residents, the city's optimism is reflected in its new vision, mission, values, and a robust strategic plan to take it forward.

Now Stunson and the city have embarked on a formal continuous improvement effort using the criteria in Florida's Sterling Award.[12] He sees meeting these criteria as the engine to propel the city forward and support the process improvements the city must make internally to achieve its strategic goals. Although he says "we're taking it small bites at a time," the results are already obvious in the city's documented successes.

In 2006, the International City/County Management Association gave its Career Excellence Award to Stunson. The association fosters excellence in local governance and recognized Stunson for "his outstanding efforts to foster representative democracy by enhancing the effectiveness of local elected officials and by consistently initiating creative and successful programs." Consistent, continuous improvement and strategic leadership work.

Failure to Improve is Not an Option

Each contemporary leader interviewed understood this dictum. Each implemented it in a way that resonated with the culture of the organization. Madison and the other framers understood the necessity for a workable amendment process, based on their unhappy experience with the un-amendable Articles of Confederation. But even Madison, who was primarily responsible for pushing through the passage of the Bill of Rights, did not understand the full power of those first ten amendments. Improvement often works that way.

Small improvements can have large impacts down the line. For example, a team in another corrugated products manufacturing company (not profiled here), designed a new process that cut fifteen minutes off the set-up time for the most critical machine. Not only were machine operations more efficient, but the action also avoided over $100,000 per year in set-up time costs (even more, in today's dollars). Later, the company realized the change had significantly increased capacity, enabling them to take on more work. As everyone in the company began to look at improvements in this new light of importance, the ripples from those "fifteen minutes" continued for a long time.

This sort of impact is documented over and over in books, professional journals, the media, and elsewhere. Strategic leaders quickly turn to making mission-critical processes more effective and efficient. Even though leaders often start with an eye toward cost-cutting, most discover that improvement is more sophisticated than that. As processes are less cumbersome and as more people are engaged, the culture and climate within the organization begin to change. People start looking for more improvements on their own. Positive results build greater enthusiasm, leading to even more accomplishments.

The Law of Unintended Good Consequences

When the framers designed a viable amendment process for the Constitution and Madison reluctantly agreed to push through a Bill of Rights in the newly formed Congress, they were not fully aware of the long-term consequences. The Bill of Rights and subsequent amendments/improvements, such as those that ended slavery and enfranchised women, youth, and minorities, have allowed the consciousness of citizens to evolve and change, so the country's vision and mission can move closer to fulfillment. "All men [and women] are created equal" was a dream in 1787. Today it is closer to fulfillment than ever, and as people continue around that spiral staircase, each new improvement moves us closer to "a more perfect union."

As modern leaders attempt to perfect their companies and organizations, what is strategic leadership? What characteristics mark leaders as strategic? What traits should leaders focus on as they work to continuously improve their own performance?

Postscript

What is Strategic Leadership?

Anyone looking back at the framers will be struck by two shared characteristics. Despite their very different personalities, backgrounds, professions, and talents, they all were visionaries who could get things done. This combination of talents is not common. Some visionary leaders never quite pull off the execution. Other leaders do a lot, but have no clear direction beyond completing the next milestone. They cannot take the organization into the future. Most of the contemporary leaders discussed in this book share that rare combination of vision and execution. When these modern leaders were asked to choose the founder or framer they admired most and who exemplified strategic leadership best, many selected George Washington.

The General: A Model of Strategic Leadership

George Washington illustrates the visionary who can act to make the vision a reality.[1] As a powerful leader devoted to the republican cause, he put his life on the line during the Revolution. But as the new nation struggled and floundered in the years following the peace treaty with the British, he became more and more convinced another, equally revolutionary change was necessary to secure a stable and effective republican government. Agreeing to attend the Constitutional Convention was a risk to his carefully guarded reputation, especially if the meeting failed or precipitated an even bigger crisis. His fellow delegates immediately acknowledged his leadership skills and unanimously elected him president of the Convention.

Because Washington did not like to speak publicly and

because he usually followed his own advice of restraint of "tongues or pens,"[2] he has been depicted by a few historians more as an affable, dumb jock, not a particularly intelligent or thoughtful leader. These depictions are no closer to the truth than the fawning, apocryphal story of young George cutting down the cherry tree and claiming, "I cannot tell a lie."

Washington is an admirable leader people can learn from precisely because he was a complex human being. He could be prickly, thin-skinned, and aloof. He made bad decisions. Yet the executives interviewed for this book recognized his outstanding leadership ability and his sense of duty. When his country needed him, he always answered the call, no matter what his personal preferences. Modern leaders have much to learn from his lifelong struggle to keep his own demons at bay as he acted in accordance with his ideals more often than not.

Always embarrassed by his lack of formal education, which ended with grade school, Washington constantly read and studied a wide range of subjects, and surrounded himself with advisors who were intellectual giants, such as Hamilton and Madison. He often used these men as ghostwriters, but they were always conveying *his* thoughts and beliefs. His trusted advisors did not *think* for him. Succinctly stated, Washington's republican philosophy was his guiding vision.

> The power under the constitution will always be in the people. It is entrusted for certain defined purposes, and for a certain limited period, to representatives of their own choosing; and whenever it is executed contrary to their interests, or not agreeable to their wishes, their servants can, and undoubtedly will be, recalled.[3]

After his inauguration as president of the United States, Washington proceeded to put his republican vision into practice. Probably no other leader could have led that transitional government from post-revolutionary chaos to an established, constitution-based republic. He literally had to invent the presidency, from the most trivial to the most significant and far-reaching details, knowing history was watching his every move. One of the reasons contemporary leaders find him so compelling was this courage to take on a huge challenge without a roadmap.

As president, Washington relied on Alexander Hamilton's financial expertise to create a stable economic system, and on Madison's political expertise to create the legislative support for his policies. Like contemporary successful leaders, Washington listened to his team's advice, made his own evaluation, and delegated responsibility and authority to them to implement his decisions.

Just as he did at the end of the Revolution, he put his republican beliefs into action when he stepped away from power after two terms as president. Even though a strengthening opposition to his policies had grown during his second term, most historians agree he could have been elected over and over for the rest of his life. Some contemporaries even wanted him to serve as the elected king for life. He refused, and stuck to his republican values and vision.

Effective Leaders Harness Their Drivers

Washington would probably have been fascinated with the work of David McClelland,[4] a pioneering psychologist, who studied what he called the acquired needs or drivers of human behavior: power, achievement, and affiliation. McClelland believed one of these three needs strongly influenced behavioral choices at any given point in a person's life.

McClelland further described the power need as having two forms; personal and social. When a person seeks to direct another's actions, personal power dominates action. In a person who seeks to organize a group of people to achieve the organization's goals, social power dominates.

McClelland defined people who sought to excel above all others and overcome all obstacles as those driven by the need for achievement. People who primarily need to build harmonious relationships he labeled as driven by affiliation needs.

The Hay Group continued McClelland's work, researching the implications for effective leadership. The researchers marked the phenomenal rise of achievement-driven leaders, the decline of power-driven leaders, and the relative stability in the number of affiliation-driven leaders over the last decade.[5] Hay Group also defined six leadership styles and correlated these with the three needs defined by McClelland.[6]

At IBM, Hay Group conducted an in-depth study of the relationship among leadership style, organizational climate, and business results. "Climate" assesses a variety of factors affecting how employees feel about working in their immediate work group, not the entire organization. Climate measures elements directly impacting people's ability to get their jobs done.[7]

The findings of the study at IBM were striking. The senior managers who had the highest performing divisions in terms of revenue also had the most energizing work climate reported by employees. The poorest performing senior managers had either neutral or demotivating climates.

Both effective and less effective senior managers had relatively high scores for achievement needs. Yet the more effective senior managers were twice as likely to have strong needs in the affiliation and power categories as were the ineffective ones.

The effective leaders were also twice as likely to score high on the visionary leadership style scale as their less effective counterparts. According to Hay Group, the visionary leadership style "is authoritative...the leader gains employees' support by clearly expressing their challenges and responsibilities in the context of the organization's overall direction and strategy."[8]

Another difference surfaced between the effective and less effective senior managers. The latter were much more likely to have what the researchers described as a pacesetting leadership style, characterized by setting the bar high, acting as a role model, and expecting everyone else to achieve at that very high level. This combination of high achievement needs and the pacesetting leadership style tends to be overly demanding and judgmental. These managers squelch creativity, participation, and energy among employees, even at high levels in the organization.

Based on these findings, new executive leadership at IBM set out to change the corporate culture. Because they wanted to improve bottom-line performance, they focused on creating an energizing climate and helped all managers become more flexible in their leadership styles.

When Hay Group measured the results from the new approach, it concluded, "a high achievement drive is still a source of strength. But companies must learn when to draw on it and when to rein it in. The challenge for managers today, then, is to return some of the balance McClelland advised." In practical terms, this means the leaders build a culture where they help the group focus on common goals, keeping the leaders' achievement needs in control.[9]

Like the most successful founders of the U.S. and contemporary executives, leaders must understand their own motivations, balancing their needs for achievement, affiliation, and power. At the same time, they must focus on the needs of the people in their organization and understand human psychology, including individual motivation. Successful leaders demonstrate flexibility and insight and have realistic expectations.

Effective Leaders are Emotionally Intelligent

Daniel Goleman, a student of McClelland, pioneered the understanding of Emotional Intelligence.[10] He found the visionary, or what he calls the authoritative leadership style, has the most significant positive impact on corporate culture. The pacesetting style has the most negative effect.[11] The authoritative leader "mobilizes people toward a vision."

Visionary/authoritative leaders say, "Come with me," and are self-confident, empathetic, and catalysts for change.[12]

McClelland, Hay Group, and Goleman all found effective leaders have learned to flex their styles, whether through coaching, self-development, or because they were born with ability to adapt readily to the needs of the situation. Goleman pointed out that no matter how flexible the person, the authoritative/visionary style was the most useful when the situation called for creating a culture supportive of a new vision. His findings are in line with what the leaders interviewed in this book reported. Goleman writes,[13]

> The authoritative leader is a visionary, he motivates people by making clear to them how their work fits into a larger vision for the organization. People who work for such leaders understand that what they do matters and why. Authoritative leadership also maximizes commitment to the organization's goals and strategy. By framing the individual tasks within a grand vision, the authoritative leader defines standards that revolve around that vision. When he gives performance feedback – whether positive or negative – the singular criterion is whether or not that performance furthers the vision... An authoritative leader states the end but generally gives people plenty of leeway to devise their own means. Authoritative leaders give people the freedom to innovate, experiment, and take calculated risks.

Goleman pointed out the necessity of building a leadership team of diverse talents and styles because no one person possesses them all in abundance. He concludes, "The business environment is continually changing, and a leader must respond in kind...executives must play their leadership styles like a pro – using the right one at just the right time and in the right measure. The payoff is in the results."[14]

The Payoff is in the Results
– Daniel Goleman

Leaders are judged on whether or not they get results. As Hay Group studies concluded,[15] companies with an energizing climate outperformed the Standard & Poor's 500 with a shareholder return of just over four percent, as compared to about one-half of one percent. Seventy percent of organizational climate is created by the leader's style in motivation and communication. Senior managers who created energized climates had profits in one year of $711 million (or twelve percent) more than those who created neutral or demotivating climates. The "great CEOs" who created positive company climates led them to an average sixty-three percent growth while the "good" CEOs demonstrated only twenty-four percent growth.[16]

Visionary, Authoritative Leaders = Successful Strategic Leaders

In this book, you met contemporary strategic leaders who have the ability to turn their vision into concrete results. The stories of these executives and their results mirror quite closely those in more scientific studies by Gallup, Goleman, and Hay Group. Strategic leaders, visionary and authoritative leaders, get great results by energizing the workforce.

For example, Ben Baldanza, president and CEO of Spirit Airlines, was cited by the *South Florida Business Journal* as one of the 2008 People to Watch. "The company has grown ten percent, with most revenue coming from its international routes...more than twenty Caribbean and Central America destinations and Mexico...Projected airline traffic for 2007 was 2,549,536 up from 1,631,382 passengers in 2006."[17]

As Baldanza lays out the dimensions of the "New Spirit Plan" he formulated, he says to "think of it like a mission on steroids."[18] It sets a vision and goals in five areas: "great service and proud of it; investing to build revenue; no one beats our costs; defensible and stable franchise; and the best place to work in the airline business." In building this strategy, Baldanza wanted to see Fort Lauderdale-Hollywood International Airport as a bigger international player. The results he achieved show Spirit is on its way.

"I work a lot at trying to create a good environment for people to excel. That means hiring the right people, helping establish the right goals, helping people get excited about being held accountable to those goals, and delivering on those goals," Baldanza reports. He spends much of his time talking with employees at every level, gives his personal, internal e-mail address to everyone, and responds to every employee's inquiry. Although he makes the final decision, he makes sure everyone can give him feedback because, "I don't like 'yes' men." Baldanza says he holds people accountable for achieving goals and won't tolerate poor performance. "Having a positive atmosphere and having good, open, honest communications and clear direction are not inconsistent with managing people's performance well. In fact, I think it's consistent with that."

Perhaps the best example of how Baldanza's successful strategic leadership style builds an energizing climate is an exchange that took place just before an interview. His administrative assistant spontaneously announced, "He's the best boss I've ever worked for, and I've been in the business a long time!"

**One Man [or Woman] of Tolerable Abilities
May Work Great Changes**
– **Ben Franklin**

Most great strategic leaders do not limit their talent and energy to their own organizations. Almost all of them become involved in their communities to find ways to improve them.

The framers applied their considerable talents to make a positive difference in the world around them. James Madison agreed to become a member of the Board of Visitors of Thomas Jefferson's new University of Virginia. Madison promised he would continue Jefferson's vision of a new type of education after his friend's death. Alexander Hamilton was a founding member of a society to free slaves and stayed active in that cause until his untimely death. Perhaps none of the founding fathers exhibited this involvement more than the indefatigable Ben Franklin.

Franklin expressed his philosophy in his *Autobiography*. He "thought that one Man of tolerable Abilities may work great Changes, and Accomplish great Affairs among Mankind, if he first forms a good Plan and...makes the Execution of that same Plan his sole Study and Business."[19] Franklin not only pulled together some like-minded souls in his Junto organization, but also created many institutions on his own, often staying behind the scenes.

Franklin approached each of his endeavors the same way. First he observed some problem people faced in their daily lives. Next, he wrote a pamphlet or article outlining the need and the solution. These were designed to energize others, whether public officials or private citizens, to get involved and donate money. Then he allowed the new organization to grow and take on a life of its own. His efforts led to the formation of fire brigades, schools and a university, hospitals, lending libraries, a philosophical society, street paving and cleaning services, insurance associations, police patrols, and post office reform.

Franklin's inventions grew out of the same keen observations of daily frustrations. For example, the smokiness of stoves of the period was a constant problem, so he invented the Franklin stove, which had a system of baffles to reduce smoke. Other inventions ranged from his famous lightening rod and bifocal glasses to musical instruments, a urinary catheter, a storage battery, swimming pads, and a mechanical arm.[20]

Stephanie Sonnabend, co-CEO of Sonesta Hotels, is an admirer of Franklin and also exemplifies his community involvement spirit. Like most talented leaders, she often takes on a leadership position in her community work. In addition to serving on boards of for-profit companies, she serves as a trustee and as a member of the executive committee of the New England Conservatory of Music in Boston, where she chairs the strategic planning committee. More recently, she has joined the Board of Overseers of Boston's Beth Israel Deaconess Medical Center. She also launched a nonprofit, Youth Microcredit International, with her son and other young people. The group's mission is to create high school ambassadors who make a difference. "We saw how lending small amounts of money to people in developing countries worked firsthand. It's so wonderful that young people understand this whole idea and how important it is."

John Zumwalt, CEO of PBS&J, the engineering firm, said his company's founders were "walking with the community leaders." When he entered the corporation's leadership ranks, he created that sort of involvement as one pillar of the company's growth strategy. He wanted to move the firm from "just being physically *in* a community to being an integral part of it; to be involved with civic leaders." Zumwalt is passionate about seeing engineers involved and "as prominent as we can be outside of our profession. We're grooming community professionals who are trusted advisors. We're spending a lot of time developing the leadership aspect of our culture."

Zumwalt was not content just to push this community commitment in his own company.

> I've spent a lot of time with statewide business organizations like the Florida Chamber of Commerce, the Florida Council of 100, and Enterprise Florida, [a public-private partnership devoted to economic development.] Often I was the only engineer in the room. But that's really what we want to do; become involved. When I was president of the Florida Engineering Society, I developed the same approach for the state's engineers to bring them up to be community professionals.

For years, they had wanted to improve their image. I asked, 'What do you want to improve it with?' I created a leadership institute to teach them how to reach beyond our industry. It was wildly successful because it was just what engineers had been waiting for. They developed a new tag line, 'to become top community professionals.'[21]

Zumwalt's tenure as president of the state engineering society energized the organization. His assessment: "I think it was because we gave it a compelling mission and we got people excited about it and membership started to skyrocket."

A few years ago, Ryder System's Greg Swienton was asked to speak at a local college commencement. He wanted to encourage the graduates to become involved in their own communities. As he thought about what he might tell the graduates, who were thirty years his junior, he realized many of them came from immigrant families. His message crystallized:

> We're all basically immigrants. I guess I'm the great patriot I am because I'm the second generation to be born in this country. My grandfather came from Poland. My dad didn't go to college. Like me, these students are the first ones to get a college degree. Just like them, I lived at home and worked to afford to go to school. I believe in the opportunity in this country.
>
> That's why I have such a high regard for this country and the freedom it offers; free enterprise, liberty, freedom of speech and religion...all of it. That's why it's a great place and that's why we have to protect it.
>
> And, you have to have balance in your life. You have to be dedicated to your faith, to your family, and to your country. You can't let any job be a detriment to that. In fact, if you get off that path of balance, you can't even do your job as well. Balance makes you more effective.

The final thing I told them was this: you have to do what is right, even when others are misinterpreting it. For me, this is a strong connection with the founding fathers. These were guys with their lives on the line. They would either hang together or hang as individuals. So you have to 'hang in there' and act on your beliefs.

Perhaps no one of the leaders that we interviewed exemplifies Franklin's spirit of community service more than Evan Rees, former president of CNL Bank. Rees always took a genuine interest in improving his community by supporting small businesses and participating actively in a number of civic and business organizations. Now, after a long and successful career in banking, he is spending his time raising significant funds for the Community Partnership for the Homeless and the Boy Scouts. His excitement is palpable as he begins applying his talents to his new endeavor. "I'm another brick in the building, but when we finish the $15 million fundraising project to rebuild the two [Boy Scout] camps destroyed by hurricanes, we'll have two of the best camps in the U.S. and be able to serve thirty-five thousand campers. This will be the most important event in the hundred-year history of scouting in South Florida. With the homeless partnership, I'm introducing new businesses to them. It's wonderful to be part of a business model for homeless issues that's a blueprint for other cities."

You Need to Stand Up and be Counted...
Take a Heroic Stance
— Michael Howe, former CEO, MinuteClinic

The contemporary leaders you met in this book all faced great challenges. They rose to meet them through an effective combination of vision and execution. They exemplify the visionary/authoritative leader who "gains employees' support by clearly expressing their challenges and responsibilities in the context of the organization's overall direction and strategy."[22] These men and women faced the same sorts of challenges encountered by leaders of all organizations. They made the difference for their organizations between success and the status quo; between moving forward or slipping backward. Each of these leaders made mistakes. What distinguishes them from unsuccessful leaders is their universal reaction to their own mistakes and those of others. The particulars of their individual situations are different but the lessons for contemporary leaders are universal: admit you are wrong, act to fix things, accept the consequences, and learn a lesson to avoid the same mistake in the future.

Both the contemporary and historic leaders profiled practiced the visionary/authoritative leadership style, inspiring employees to get results. Michael Howe, the former CEO of MinuteClinic, expressed what this model of leadership is all about:

> The key thing that differentiates great leaders is empathy. Of course you have to have intellect, vision, communication skills, and all those things. And I'm not talking about the squishy side of being kind and sweet all the time. I'm talking about being able to see inside the folks who are on your staff, to understand their skills and capacities. Then you have to be tuned in to how they are reacting to the situation.
>
> When I became president of Arby's, I just loved it. I loved being responsible, being accountable. It's funny. The passion doesn't come from control as much as it does from the ability to expect things from people and watch them deliver.
>
> The paradox to me is that, as your responsibility grows, your control collapses along with your rights. You

don't have a right to come in and scream at people. You don't have a right to be abusive. You don't have a right to decide not to show up at a meeting. You don't have a right not to deliver on your commitment. You don't have the right to behave poorly, to choose your stock option price, to spend the company's money on personal excess. You lose those 'rights' when you take on responsibilities.

The higher up the ladder you go, the more negative the impact that your behavior can have. You have to be consistent in your behavior, or people will become neurotic and the organization will collapse because people don't know what to expect.

The attitude you need to go through life is to have something you really believe in. Then you need to stand up and be counted...to take an almost heroic stance.

Conventional Wisdom is Not So Conventional

Although this uncommon ability to combine the abstract and the practical is admirable, the leaders you met in this book are not presented as perfect leaders to be emulated blindly. Learn from their savvy and success as well as their failures and foibles. The *Conventional Wisdom* captured from the framers and modern leaders is best summed up by these passages written long ago by George Washington:

I walk on untrodden ground. There is scarcely any part of my conduct which may not hereafter be drawn into precedent.[23]

We must never despair; our situation has been compromising before, and it changed for the better; so I trust it will again. If difficulties arise, we must put forth new exertion and proportion out efforts to exigencies of the times.[24]

It is a wonder to me, there should be found a single monarch, who does not realize that his own glory and felicity must depend on the prosperity and happiness of his People.[25]

If after all my humble but faithful endeavors to advance the felicity of my Country and mankind, I may indulge a hope that my labours have not been altogether without success, it will be the only real compensation I can receive in the closing of life.[26]

If there was ever a time when every organization needed strategic leadership, it is now. Whether in a small city, a global corporation, a public hospital, a manufacturer, or a regional bank, executives and managers are called on to face potentially crushing pressures. Many will succumb or choose so-called safe remedies. A few leaders will emerge from the crucible of economic chaos with the courage to take revolutionary action.

Like the Constitutional framers, they will define a future and persist in translating that desired state into reality. They will not give in to short-term expediency. They will cast themselves in the mold of the framers as visionary, authoritative, and strategic leaders. They will learn from their mistakes and from history. They will inspire a new generation of leaders by their example because they are ordinary people doing the extraordinary. They will mentor new generations of leaders who reject the clichés of business as usual. They will sow the seeds for a new, dominant style of leadership that transforms every organization where it is practiced, from the smallest micro business to the top echelons of government.

The option is yours. Find your own *Conventional Wisdom*; become a strategic leader who energizes people, and unflinchingly brings your vision to life. Walk in the footsteps of the framers. Establish your own 'more perfect' organization.

Chapter End Notes

Author's Foreword

1. Ralph Ketcham, James Madison: A biography (Charlottesville, 1990), p. 376. Dolley Payne, the future Mrs. Madison, referred to him as the "great little Madison" in a note to a friend before her first date with him. "Little" because he stood about five feet, seven inches with a slender build. "Great" because of his involvement with creating the U.S. Constitution.
2. Adrienne Koch, ed., Notes of Debates in the Federal Convention of 1787 Reported by James Madison (New York, 1987), p. 3. The phrase "ancient to modern" from Madison's preface to his notes, is repeated constantly in almost every reference to him and the Convention.
3. "Jemmy" was Madison's nickname among friends and enemies alike.

Preamble

1. Richard Norton Smith, Patriarch: George Washington and the New American Nation (Boston, 1993), p. 83.
2. Although it is standard to capitalize "Founding Fathers" and "Framers", some contemporary scholars such as Joseph Ellis have consciously used the lower case to help modern readers see these men as humans, not statues, from whom we can learn. I have adopted this approach because this is a major premise of this book.
3. Joseph Ellis, American Creation: Triumphs and Tragedies at the Founding of the Republic (New York, 2007) p. xi. [emphasis added]
4. The following companies were clients of the author's company, Advantage Leadership, Inc.: City of Coral Gables, Gibraltar Private Bank and Trust, York

Container Company, Novelty Manufacturing.
5. David Brown announced his retirement as city manager in October 2008 and resigned in November, as this book went to press.
6. Tony Caron retired in 2007.
7. As this book was going to press, Michael Howe left MinuteClinic and founded his own consulting firm.
8. This fictional dialogue is derived from many historical sources to recreate the flavor of the situation and discussion at the time.
9. Willard Sterne Randall, Thomas Jefferson: A Life (New York, 1993), p. 482. This statement of Jefferson's about Shays Rebellion is widely quoted, often out of context.
10. Edward Mead Earle, ed., The Federalist: A Commentary on the Constitution of the United States (New York, 1937), p. 59. The constitutional framers' vision was articulated in the Declaration of Independence. Their strategy was to create a republican form of government to make 'life, liberty and the pursuit of happiness' a reality. The founders used the word 'republican' as James Madison defined it in The Federalist No. 10: "a government in which the scheme of representation takes place...delegation of the government...to a small number of citizens elected by the rest...to refine and enlarge the public views, by passing them through the medium of a chosen body of citizens, whose wisdom may best discern the true interest of their country, and whose patriotism and love of justice will be least likely to sacrifice it to temporary or partial considerations."
11. New York's delegation rules required at least two of the three members to be present to decide how to cast the state's one vote. Each state had one vote as in the Confederation Congress.
12. Adrienne Koch, ed. Notes of Debates in the Federal Convention of 1787 Reported by James Madison (New York, 1987), p. 23.

13. Ibid., p. 24.

Article I: Deal With the Real

1. Adrienne Koch, ed. James Madison, Notes of Debates in the Federal Convention of 1787 Reported by James Madison (New York, 1987), p. 28
2. Ibid.
3. Rhode Island refused to send delegates.
4. Jim Collins, Good To Great, (New York, 2001). The phrase "face the brutal facts" from the book was quoted by Hayworth and his team regularly after they read and discussed the book together at their monthly meetings.
5. Alexander Hamilton, Benjamin Franklin, Gouverneur Morris, John Adams, John Jay, and others worked hard to bring about the convention. They had to proceed gingerly. Those for whom the status quo was just fine, especially many members of the existing Confederation Congress and most state politicians, would never have sanctioned a meeting to overthrow the Articles of Confederation.
6. Edward Mead Earle, ed., The Federalist: A Commentary on the Constitution of the United States (New York, 1937). Madison, along with Alexander Hamilton and John Jay, wrote a series of essays defending the Constitution under the collective pen name Publius.

Article II: Bring Vision to Reality

1. Oscar Corral, "UM funding drive nets a record $1.4 billion," The Miami Herald, Feb. 9, 2008.
2. Ibid.
3. Akhil Reed Amar, America's Constitution: A Biography, (New York, 2005).
4. Jefferson's Republican Party later became the Democratic Republican Party, and later dropped

Republican to become the predecessor of today's Democratic Party, which ironically now embraces a larger central government with less power for the states.
5. The Federalist Party faded from the scene in the first decade of the nineteenth century. Although today's Republican Party, founded just before the Civil War, maintains the Federalists' emphasis on strong national defense and a pro-business policy, it champions smaller government and more rights for the states.
6. John Ferling, Adams vs. Jefferson: The Tumultuous Election of 1800 (New York, 2004).
7. Michael Howe is still actively involved in promoting his vision for health care.
8. The Malcolm Baldrige National Quality Award recognizes companies' commitments to world-class quality and results (http://www.quality.nist.gov). Florida created the Sterling Award (http://www.floridasterling.com), based on the Baldrige, to honor state-based entities which demonstrate excellence.
9. See a variety of accounts in these and other sources: Joseph Ellis, Founding Brothers: The Revolutionary Generation (New York, 2000); Joseph Ellis, His Excellency: George Washington (New York, 2004); Gordon Wood, Revolutionary Characters: What Made the Founders Different (New York, 2006); Gore Vidal, Inventing a Nation: Washington, Adams, Jefferson (New Haven, 2003); Peter Henriques, Realistic Visionary: A Portrait of George Washington (Charlottesville, 2006); Richard Norton Smith, Patriarch: George Washington and the New American Nation (New York, 1993).

Article III: Get People on a Mission

1. To learn more about Gouverneur Morris: William Howard Adams, Gouverneur Morris: An Independent Life, (New Haven, 2003).

2. The actual quote is, "First, I believe that this nation should commit itself to achieving the goal, before the decade is out, of landing a man on the moon and returning him safely to earth." President John Kennedy's Special Message to the Congress on Urgent National Needs. May 25, 1961 http://millercenter.org/scripps/archive/speeches/detail/3368.
3. Marcus Buckingham and Curt Coffman, First Break All the Rules: What the World's Greatest Managers Do Differently (New York, 1999).
4. Rodd Wagner and James Harter, 12: The Elements of Great Managing (New York, 2006).
5. Ibid., p. 114.
6. Ibid., p. 112. [Emphasis added.]
7. Hospital Corporation of America is one of the leading health care providers, operating 168 hospitals and 113 outpatient centers in the U.S. and England, with revenues of $27 billion.
8. Ellen Forman, "Broward's Healthcare Challenges," FloridaTrend.com, January 1, 2008.
9. Joint Commission on Accreditation of Healthcare Organizations
10. "Broward Health loses CEO to Louisiana," SouthFloridaBizJournals.com, (January 8, 2008).
11. Ibid.
12. Ibid.
13. Ibid.
14. Mark Scott, "How Alan Levine transformed the culture at Broward Health by developing strong bonds with his employees," sbnonline.com/Local/Article/13714/67/0/Medicine_man. (2008).
15. Forman.
16. Ibid.
17. Scott.

18. Anthony Man "Alan Levine resigns as president of North Broward Hospital District," Sun-Sentinal.com, (January 9, 2008).
19. Ibid.
20. "Broward Health loses CEO to Louisiana," SouthFloridaBizJournals.com, (January 8, 2008).

Article IV: The Road Re-Traveled

1. Adrienne Koch, ed. Notes of Debates in the Federal Convention of 1787 Reported by James Madison (New York, 1987), p. 28.
2. Bob King, Hoshin Planning: The Development Approach (Methuen, Massachusetts, 1989) Chapters 1-11.
3. Robert Kaplan and David Norton, The Balanced Scorecard: Translating Strategy into Action (Boston, 1996), p. 9.
4. King, Chapters 1-3.
5. James Hutson, ed., *Supplement to Max Farrand's The Records of the Federal Convention of 1787* (New Haven, 1987), p. 34.
6. Ibid., p. 144.
7. Ibid., p. 256.
8. Special Independence National Park Archives Services Bicentennial Constitutional Convention Day Book Research Project Work Files (Philadelphia, 1987). Remarks attributed to William Paterson's letter to his wife of July 17, 1787.
9. Max Farrand, The Framing of the Constitution of the United States (New Haven,1913), p. 93.
10. Koch, pp. 25-26.
11. Ibid., p. 28.
12. Hutson, p. 236.
13. Farrand, pp. 94-95.
14. Ibid., pp. 105-107.

Article V: Mistakes Were Made

1. Lee Iacocca, Where Have All the Leaders Gone? (New York, 2007), p. 137.
2. Quotations of George Washington (Bedford, Massachusetts, 2003), p.14. [Emphasis added.]
3. Each elector cast two votes without designating which was preferred for President and which for Vice President. The result was a tie in the 1800 election pitting John Adams against Thomas Jefferson. The tie threw the decision into the House of Representatives, which took thirty-six rounds of voting to pick Jefferson. The situation was rectified in the Twelfth Amendment, which instructs electors to designate which candidate will receive their vote for President and which for Vice President.
4. Luda Kopeikina, The Right Decision Every Time: How to Reach Perfect Clarity on Tough Decisions (Upper Saddle River, 2005), pp.159 ff.
5. It was the author's decision to conceal identities when providing these examples of mistakes. The point is to illustrate common frames, not expose the foibles of leaders with a positive record. Thoughtful leaders will ask themselves whether they have similar fames that lead them to bad decisions. Some of the interviewed leaders made some rather public mistakes, which are not discussed here. The point is not to judge but expose frames, learn from them, and improve decision making.
6. Kopeikina, pp. 170 ff.
7. Quotations, p. 9. [Emphasis added.]
8. Akhil Reed Amar, *America's Constitution: A Biography,* (New York, 2005), pp. 264-5.
9. Christopher Collier and James Lincoln Collier, Decision in Philadelphia: The Constitutional Convention of 1787 (New York, 1986), p. 221. See Chapters 15 and 16 for a fuller discussion of the compromises and behind-the-scenes maneuvering.

10. Here we are only using one example of bad decisions through "framing." The issue of the treatment of Native Americans in the Constitution and afterwards is discussed in the latest work from Joseph Ellis, American Creation: Triumphs and Tragedies at the Founding of the Republic (New York, 2007).
11. Catherine Drinker Bowen, Miracle at Philadelphia: The Story of the Constitutional Convention May to September 1787 (Boston, 1986), p. 200.
12. Adrienne Koch, ed. Notes of Debates in the Federal Convention of 1787 Reported by James Madison (New York, 1987), pp. 409 ff. These debates are extensively edited to give a flavor of the debate.
13. The content of these debates has come from Koch. I've edited and paraphrased it to read like first-person debate, modernized spelling and some words, added the 'staging' elements to recreate the dramatic discussions, and altered the sequences to create a more dramatic and understandable flow of ideas.
14. Koch, pp. 409-412.
15. Taxes on exports would fall most heavily on the slave states' exports of tobacco, rice, and indigo.
16. David Stewart provides an excellent new treatment of these debates in his book published after much of this book was written. David O. Stewart, The Summer of 1787: The Men Who Invented the Constitution (New York, 2007.)
17. Koch, p. 502.
18. Stewart has an insightful discussion of this point.
19. Amalgamated and Apex are pseudonyms for two former client companies not discussed in this book.
20. Koch, pp. 503-508.
21. Koch, pp. 504-505.
22. Amar, pp. 252-258.
23. Ralph Ketcham, James Madison: A Biography (Charlottesville, 1990), p. 625.

24. Ibid., pp. 626-629.
25. Amar, pp. 268 ff.
26. Andrew Levy, The First Emancipator: Slavery, Religion, and the Quiet Revolution of Robert Carter (New York, 2005), p. xi. Levy's extensive compelling biography of Robert Carter III brings to light a forgotten and yet key player in the history of slavery. It is a tantalizingly different frame for dealing with the issue in the late eighteenth century. All the subsequent discussions of Carter are based on Levy.
27. Ibid.
28. Henry Wiencek, An Imperfect God: George Washington, His Slaves, and the Creation of America (New York, 2003.)
29. Walter Isaacson, Benjamin Franklin: An American Life, (New York, 2003), pp. 462 ff.
30. Luda Kopeikina, in our discussions of The Right Decision Every Time
31. Jeff Broadwater, George Mason: Forgotten Founder (Chapel Hill, 2006), pp. 34. As the subsequent discussion makes clear, the frames for Mason and others were complex and included a fundamental racist view.
32. Ibid., p. 35.
33. Ibid., pp. 35-36.
34. Ibid.
35. Collier and Collier, p. 240.
36. Isaacson, pp. 457-8. Swienton quoted Franklin almost word for word. I have reproduced the fuller quote.
37. George Mason, Elbridge Gerry, and Edmund Randolph were the only delegates remaining until the end of the Convention who refused to sign the proposed Constitution. Randolph, Governor of Virginia, later changed his mind and supported the Constitution during the ratification battle in his state.
38. Levy, pp.194-5.

39. Rebecca Staton-Reinstein, "Engineering a Potent Business Strategy," In Focus Magazine (Jan/Feb, 2005), pp. 36-7.

Article VI: Execution is Harder than Revolution

1. Walter Isaacson, Benjamin Franklin: An American Life (New York, 2003), p. 459.
2. Each state created a specially-elected ratifying convention, separate from its legislature. Some of these special bodies were more broadly representative of the population than the existing governing structures. All ratification dates come from http://www.usconstitution.net/ratifications.html
3. Hamilton, Jay, and Madison chose the name Publius, in honor of Publius Valerius Publicola, a founder and one of the first Consuls of the first Roman Republic. The framers, all students of history, often referred to details of the evolution and demise of the Roman Republic to inform their arguments. The meaning behind the pseudonym would have been obvious to their audience.
4. Edward Mead Earle, ed., The Federalist, A Commentary on the Constitution of the United States. (New York, 1937), pp. ix-x.
5. Ibid, p. xi. Quoted from the ruling of the Supreme Court in Cohens vs. Virginia, 1821.
6. Rhode Island changed its ratification voting method.
7. Confirmed on website: http://www.gibraltarprivate.com/history.jsp.
8. See Articles I and VII of this book for a discussion of how they accomplished these goals.
9. See Article V of this book for a discussion of frames. The Gibralter case study illustrates the power of frame shifting.
10. David Brown announced his retirement as city manager in October 2008 and resigned in November, as this

book went to press.
11. Michael Hammerschmidt died from cancer in August 2008.
12. Adrienne Koch, ed. Notes on Debates in the Federal Convention of 1787 Reported by James Madison. (New York, 1987), p. 17-18.
13. Ibid., p. xii.
14. Ibid., p. xv-xvi.
15. Robert Ketcham, James Madison: A Biography (Charlottesville, 1990). The details of the ratification debate in Virginia, discussed in Chapter 11, illustrate Madison's masterful political and debating skills, under the most trying circumstances, against a powerful foe.
16. Madison and others believed the bills of rights in various states already protected people and nowhere in the Constitution were these rights denied. See *Federalist* No. 58.
17. Madison and others knew how difficult the compromises were to achieve in the Convention. They feared a new convention would undermine these fragile agreements. Madison also believed anti-Federalists would flock to a new convention and undo the federal system.

Article VII: Nurturing Human Nature

1. Edward Mead Earle, ed., The Federalist: A Commentary on the Constitution of the United States (New York, 1937), p. 337.
2. Adrienne Koch, ed., Notes of Debates in the Federal Convention of 1787 Reported by James Madison (New York, 1987), pp. 131-135.
3. Ibid., p. 52.
4. Rodd Wagner & James Harter, 12: The Elements of Great Managing (New York, 2007)
5. Henry Wiencek, An Imperfect God: George Washington, His Slaves, and the Creation of America (New York,

2003), pp. 34-40.
6. Richard Norton Smith, Patriarch: George Washington and the New American Nation (Boston,1993), 214-215.
7. As contentious as the slavery debate was, the principle delegates were not going to let the Convention fail over the issue. The political power at stake in the new national government drove each side to be willing to wreck the entire endeavor to secure the upper hand in representation.
8. Christopher Collier and James L. Collier, Decision in Philadelphia: The Constitutional Convention of 1787 (New York, 1986), p. 167.
9. Max Farrand, The Records of the Federal Convention of 1787 (New Haven, 1966), I, 500.
10. Collier, p. 168.
11. Farrand, I, 512-3.
12. For a riveting description of the entire representation debate with its political twists and turns, see Chapter 13 in the Colliers' *Decision in Philadelphia*, cited above,
13. B.W. Tuckman, "Developmental sequence in small groups," Psychological Bulletin, 63(6), (1965), 384-399.
14. Luda Kopeikina, The Right Decision Every Time: How to Reach Perfect Clarity on Tough Decisions (Upper Saddle River, 2005), pp. 2-66. [Emphasis in original.]
15. Ropes courses get their name from an activity where fully-harnessed participants climb a wall while their teammates hold the ropes that aid the climb. The courses usually involve a variety of outdoor activities aimed at building trust among team members.
16. James Hutson, ed, Supplement to Max Farrand's The Records of the Federal Convention of 1787 (New Haven, 1987), p. 121.
17. Ibid., p. 267
18. Ibid., p. 97

19. Ibid., p. 295
20. John Vile, The Constitutional Convention of 1787: A Comprehensive Encyclopedia of America's Founding (Santa Barbara, 2005), I, 214.
21. W. Edwards Deming, Out of the Crisis, (Cambridge, 1982)
22. James Madison was the last sitting president to actually execute his Commander-in-Chief role on the battlefield.
23. See Ron Chernow's *Alexander Hamilton* (New York, 2004) for a vivid description.
24. Joseph Ellis tells the story compellingly in *Founding Brothers* (New York, 2002).
25. Smith, p. 173.

Amendments

1. Gene Kranz, Failure is Not an Option (New York, 2000).
2. Elbridge Gerry is remembered today primarily in the term 'gerrymander,' based on his name. He served as James Madison's vice president from 1813-1814, and died in office.
3. Edward Mead Earle, ed., The Federalist, A Commentary on the Constitution of the United States. (New York, 1937), pp. 558-9
4. Ibid.
5. Richard Labunski, James Madison and the Struggle for the Bill of Rights (New York, 2006). A full study of Madison's pivotal role in securing the first ten amendments to the Constitution.
6. For more information on these significant contributors to the modern quality improvement movement: W. Edwards Deming, Out of the Crisis (Cambridge, Mass, 1982); W. Edwards Deming, The New Economics for Industry, Government, Education (Cambridge, Mass,

1994); Joseph M. Juran, Juran on Planning for Quality (New York, 1988); Joseph M. Juran and A. Blanton Godfrey, Juran's Quality Handbook (Milwaukee, 1999), Fifth Edition; Kaoru Ishikawa, What Is Total Quality Control? The Japanese Way (Upper Saddle River, New Jersey, 1985).
7. Six Sigma is named for the statistical concept of standard deviation or the amount of variation in any process. This variation or inconsistency leads to defects. Six Sigma can be translated to mean there are no more than 3.4 defects in every million opportunities, a very high level of quality.
8. Visit the website of the American Society for Quality for resources, http://www.asq.org.
9. The HBO original series, airing first in 2008, was based on David McCullough's *John Adams* (New York, 2001). As this book was in the production process, several of the interviewees mentioned watching the series on TV or DVD, while many had read the book. They believed there were important lessons on leadership and understanding American history for themselves and their counterparts. These lessons are discussed in Rebecca Staton-Reinstein, "Learn from History: Successful leaders are students," Leadership Excellence, 25 (11) (November 2008), 14.
10. The Continental Congress met in York for nine months from 1777-1778. This is where the ill-fated Articles of Confederation were drawn up and the words "United States" were first used.
11. Jim Collins, Good to Great: Why Some Companies Make the Leap . . . and Others Don't (New York, 2001).
12. For details visit http://www.floridasterling.com.

Postscript

1. These observations on Washington are drawn from all

of the biographies and histories cited throughout this book.
2. Quotations of George Washington (Bedford, Massachusetts, 2003), p. 9.
3. Ibid., p. 10.
4. Discussions of David McClelland's work can be found in any textbook on psychology or organizational development. For example, John R. Schermerhorn et al., *Managing Organizational Behavior* (New York: 1991), pp. 136-139.
5. Scott Sprier, Mary Fontaine, and Ruth Malloy, "Leadership Run Amok: The Destructive Potential of Overachievers," Harvard Business Review, June, 2006.
6. Six Leadership Styles: Coercive or Directive, Authoritative or Visionary, Affiliative, Democratic or Participative, Pacesetting, Coaching; described in reference by Sprier et al.
7. Eliza Glaser, Rosie de Cosmo, and Nancy Rehbine Zintis, "Leadership as a Competitive Advantage: A Best Practice Approach for Developing Leaders and Driving Business Results," (presentation to the South Florida Organizational Development Network, February 5, 2008).
8. Sprier et al.
9. Ibid.
10. Daniel Goleman, Emotional Intelligence: Why it can matter more than IQ (New York, 1997).
11. Daniel Goleman, "Leadership that Gets Results," Harvard Business Review, (March-April 2000).
12. Ibid.
13. Ibid.
14. Ibid.
15. Glaser
16. Ibid.
17. Tynisa Trapps, "Power Players Poised for Action," South

Florida Business Journal, (January 4-8, 2008), p. 11.
18. The discussion of the New Spirit Plan comes from our interviews with Baldanza.
19. Gordon Wood, The Americanization of Benjamin Franklin (New York, 2004), p. 44.
20. Walter Isaacson, Benjamin Franklin: An American Life (New York, 2003), pp. 575-6.
21. John Zumwalt is co-founder of the Florida Engineering Society/Florida Institute of Consulting Engineers Leadership Institute.
22. Spier et al.
23. Quotations, p. 20.
24. Ibid., p. 22.
25. Ibid., p. 30.
26. Ibid., p. 32.

Acknowledgements

The ideas in this book jump out of my mind onto paper with many predecessors, from idle conversation to sustained work. All of the people I acknowledge here made a major contribution.

The twenty executives who agreed to spend time talking with me and provide the modern content and insights for this book were gracious, candid, and forthcoming. They shared openly in interviews, took my calls, answered my e-mails, and were willing to chat about additional ideas and follow-up articles. They add the value of their own wisdom and experience to every idea.

The book would not have been possible without my husband, Stephen Reinstein. How can anyone devote time to a creative project without the special support of a soul mate? Steve has been my anchor throughout this long and winding journey. He's read drafts, offered ideas, and even found one of the executives I interviewed. More importantly, he's seen me through the rough patches and been there at every step. He's put up with my obsession with the historical part of the research, spending vacation time visiting historical sites and sharing me with Madison, Jefferson, and Washington. I could not have done this without him.

My incredible mastermind group, Jim Barber, Debbie Benami-Rahm, Alicia Blain, and Linda Sherwin, read and critiqued numerous drafts, gave me many ideas, and supported me at every step since 2006. In addition, Jim added his copywriting genius to my marketing efforts.

Sam Horn, former executive director of the Maui Writers Conference and its sixteen-time emcee, as well as best-selling author, served as my coach at several critical points during the long trip from idea to fruition. Her enthusiasm and encouragement made a big difference at those key junctures. She supplied the Conventional Wisdom part of the title. She was an excellent writing coach, marketing mentor, and advisor on the nuances of publishing.

Vickie Sullivan, another wonderful coach, started my search for a north star for my business, which led directly to a focus for this book as it took shape in my mind. Her encouragement and suggestions helped translate these ideas into my keynote presentations, spreading practical ideas for strategic leadership.

While working on the book, I still ran my strategic planning consulting business, and that required lots of additional work from my office manager, the "divine" Debra Upshaw. Advantage Leadership, Inc., owes much of its ongoing success to her formidable skills, support, and effort. She keeps the daily operations functioning smoothly and provides moral support at every turn.

My friend Gus Gutierrez kindly donated his fabulous country home on the Indian River as a writer's refuge. I created the chapter drafts in the weeks I spent there.

My strategic business partner and friend, Ellen Bristol, read and critiqued the work along the way and made sure I stayed on track. When I was feeling the book would never be finished or that a main concept was going nowhere, she was always there with sage advice, encouragement, and a swift kick when I needed it. We consulted as a team to several of the companies discussed in the book and her observations enriched my own.

Karen Stevens, archivist at the Independence National Historic Park in Philadelphia, was invaluable in helping me choose appropriate historical documents in my research on the Constitutional Convention. She spent time with me, found obscure references, and was ready to share everything in this remarkable facility. She made each of my visits to the archives fruitful and exciting.

I had two superb editors to create the final book, David

Kohn and Gina Carroll. In addition to their editing talents, they both love history and added their own insights and sharpened my views with their critical questions.

David Kohn actually got me going formally on this project. At a National Speakers Association chapter meeting, I won a consultation with him. He gave me strong encouragement to actually start writing this book. Later, his diligent editing helped me dump most of the jargon, squelched my tendency to jump to new topics with no transitions, and helped rescue my best writing from being buried.

Gina Carroll was always supportive as she wielded her blue pencil, caught those nasty little typos, and pointed out weak writing. She's served me well on other projects, and this one is no exception. Her willingness to be a sounding board helped me decide when to refine ideas, leave things out, and include more background.

Woodie and Tony Lesesne, publishers of In Focus Magazine, gave me the chance to write a regular column and interview business leaders. They generated new ideas for interviews and provided encouragement. The work on those interviews gave me the idea to add the views and practices of a variety of contemporary leaders to the historical material and case studies from my clients in the book.

Although many people suggested executives to interview, Barb Patterson and Romayne Berry made introductions to leaders who became integral parts of the book.

The remarkable author and coach, Lisa Jimenez, pushed and inspired me with her own enthusiasm. She told me, "The world needs this book," when I was having my doubts. She gave me a book of quotations from George Washington that inspired new ideas. Everyone at her Rich Life retreats in Paris in 2005 and Versailles in 2006 continues to give me support and encouragement.

Lilja Itenge Prieur, who participated in both retreats, has become my friend, business partner, and inspiration. Her home in Paris has been another writer's refuge for me. The mastermind retreat we created together continues to keep me on track. Her life story, which will eventually appear in book form, is an ongoing inspiration to persevere in the face of monumental odds.

At the Versailles retreat, Ford Saeks told me, "Your book is written! Just put it on paper." Ford's confident confrontation broke through my own resistance. I wrote a new chapter that day and got on track to finish the book.

Ford's company, Prime Concepts, has worked with my publisher, Tobsus Press, to coordinate all of the book design work. In addition to Ford's continuing support, working with the Prime Concepts staff has been a pleasure, as they guided the creative production process. Special kudos go to Maria Bustamante, Chad Porter, Alicia Gregg, Chad Fatino, and Jeff Sparks.

I conceived the original idea for the book cover early in the process of writing the book, but it took other talents to bring it to life. My photographer, Steve Reed, created the first iteration of the idea. He used body doubles for several of the framers to illustrate the theme that the Constitutional Convention was a strategic planning session using the same approaches modern leaders employ. Thanks to Steve Reinstein, J.B. Glossinger, and Jim Barber for filling in for the framers. (I sat in for James Madison, behind the table.) Jeff Sparks at Prime Concepts turned the idea into a striking cover.

Paris is also the home of Nan Norton, whose gracious hospitality and strategic marketing advice have been invaluable. Her efforts to promote me and my books in Paris, and to set up speaking engagements, are invaluable.

I also owe a debt to Jon Hinkamp and Joe Caccavo who, in the early 1980s, challenged me to think more seriously about what leadership actually is. They were role models and mentors. Jon also prodded me to read more history and learn its lessons.

As I described in the Author's Foreword, my parents, Ruth and Ralph Staton, were influential in instilling a love of history early in my life that remains alive today. My mother also was an English teacher; she made sure I learned the fundamentals of expressing myself, yet she went further by her example. She was a voracious reader and our home was filled with books from around the world. Even after her eyesight failed, she listened to books on tape so she could remain active in her book club. She also told wonderful stories from the Greek myths and world history to those of her own imagination. She wrote a Ph.D. and two masters' dissertations, as well as articles for the local paper. Her own literary aspirations were never fully met, but they live on in me and my daughter, Michaela, another budding writer. Michaela is always a source of pride and strength for me in all my undertakings. We encourage one another in our writing efforts, and in realizing our dreams. In turn, we're inspired by my sister, Charlotte Munning, an accomplished ceramic artist. She showed us that we can turn our own visions into reality. She is the one who convinced me that we "Staton girls" are entrepreneurs and can run successful businesses.

Finally, I thank Virginia Howard, my dear counselor, who guided me out of labyrinth of depression and helped me unleash my creativity.

Rebecca Staton-Reinstein, Ph.D.
North Miami Beach, Florida

Selected Bibliography

Achenbach, Joel. *The Grand Idea: George Washington's Potomac and the Race to the West.* New York: Simon & Schuster, 2004.

Ackerman, Bruce. *The Failure of the Founding Fathers: Jefferson, Marshall, and the Rise of Presidential Democracy.* Cambridge: Belknap Press Harvard University Press, 2005.

Adams, William Howard. *Gouverneur Morris: An Independent Life.* New Haven: Yale University Press, 2003.

Allgor, Catherine. *A Perfect Union: Dolley Madison and the Creation of the American Nation.* New York: Henry Holt and Company, 2006.

Amar, Akhil Reed. *America's Constitution: A Biography.* New York: Random House, 2005.

American Society for Quality. http://www.asq.org

Bailyn, Bernard. *To Begin the World Anew: The Genius and Ambiguities of the American Founders.* New York: Vintage Books, Random House, 2004.

Berkin, Carol. *A Brilliant Solution: Inventing the American Constitution.* Orlando: Harvest Book, Harcourt, Inc. 2002.

Boorstin, Daniel. *The Lost World of Thomas Jefferson.* Boston: Beacon Press, 1948.

Bowen, Catherine Drinker. *Miracle at Philadelphia: The Story of the Constitutional Convention May to September 1787*. Boson: Little, Brown and Company, 1986.

Breyer, Stephen. *Active Liberty: Interpreting our Democratic Constitution*. New York: Alfred Knopf, 2006.

Broadwater, Jeff. *George Mason: Forgotten Founder*. Chapel Hill: The University of North Carolina Press, 2006.

Brodie, Fawn. *Thomas Jefferson: An Intimate History*. New York: W. W. Norton & Company, 1974.

Brookhiser, Richard. *What Would the Founders Do?* New York: Basic Books, 2006.

"Broward Health loses CEO to Louisiana," http://www.SouthFloridaBizJournals.com, (January 8, 2008).

Buckingham, Marcus and Curt Coffman. *First Break All the Rules: What the World's Greatest Managers Do Differently*. New York: Simon & Schuster, 1999.

Burns, Eric. *Infamous Scribblers: The Founding Fathers and the Rowdy Beginnings of American Journalism*, New York: Public Affairs, 2006.

Cerami, Charles. *Young Patriots: The Remarkable Story of Two Men, their Impossible Plan and the Revolution that Created the Constitution*. Naperville, Illinois: Sourcebooks, Inc., 2005.

Chernow, Ron. *Alexander Hamilton*. New York: Penguin Press, 2004.

Collier, Christopher, and James L. Collier. *Decision in*

Philadelphia: The Constitutional Convention of 1787. New York: Ballantine Books, 1986.

Collins, Jim. *Good to Great: Why Some Companies Make the Leap . . . and Others Don't*. New York: HarperBusiness, 2001.

Constitution Ratification Dates. http://www.usconstitution.net/ratifications.html.

Corral, Oscar, "UM funding drive nets a record $1.4 billion," The Miami Herald, (Feb. 9, 2008).

Deming, W. Edwards. *Out of the Crisis*. Cambridge: MIT Center for Advanced Engineering Study, 1982.

———. *The New Economics for Industry, Government, Education*. Cambridge: MIT CAES, 1994.

Earle, Edward Mead, ed. *The Federalist: A Commentary on the Constitution of the United States*. New York: The Modern Library, 1937.

Ellis, Joseph. *After the Revolution: Profiles of Early American Culture*. New York: W. W. Norton & Company, 1979.

———. *American Sphinx: The Character of Thomas Jefferson*. New York: Vintage Books, Random House, 1998.

———. *Founding Brothers: The Revolutionary Generation*. New York: Vintage Books, Random House, 2002.

———. *His Excellency: George Washington*. New York: Alfred Knopf, 2004.

———. *Patriots: Brotherhood of the American Revolution.* Barnes & Noble Audio, 2004.

———. *American Creation: Triumphs and Tragedies at the Founding of the Republic.* New York: Alfred A. Knopf, 2007.

Farrand, Max *The Records of the Federal Convention of 1787.* New Haven: Yale University Press, 1966, 3 volumes.

———. *The Framing of the Constitution of the United States.* New Haven: Yale University Press, 1913.

Ferling, John. *Setting the World Ablaze: Washington, Adams, Jefferson, and the American Revolution.* New York: Oxford University Press, 2000.

———. *Adams vs. Jefferson: The Tumultuous Election of 1800.* New York: Oxford University Press, 2004.

———. *A Leap in the Dark: The Struggle to Create the American Republic.* New York: Oxford University Press, 2003.

Florida Sterling Award. http://www.floridasterling.com.

Forman, Ellen "Broward's Healthcare Challenges," http://www.FloridaTrend.com, (January 1, 2008)

Franklin, Benjamin. *Autobiography.* Roslyn, New York: Walter J. Black, 1941.

Gilman, Daniel. *James Monroe.* New York: Chelsea House, 1983. (American Statesmen Series).

Glaser, Eliza, Rosie de Cosmo, and Nancy Rehbine Zintis. "Leadership as a Competitive Advantage: A Best Practice Approach for Developing Leaders and Driving Business

Results." Presentation, South Florida Organizational Development Network, February 5, 2008.

Goleman, Daniel. *Emotional Intelligence: Why it can matter more than IQ*. New York: Bantam Books, 1997.

———. "Leadership that Gets Results," *Harvard Business Review*, (March-April 2000),78-90.

Hendrickson, David. *Peace Pact: The Lost World of the American Founding*. Lawrence: University Press of Kansas, 2003.

Henriques, Peter. *Realistic Visionary: A Portrait of George Washington*. Charlottesville: University of Virginia Press, 2006.

Hutson, James, ed. *Supplement to Max Farrand's The Records of the Federal Convention of 1787*. New Haven: Yale University Press, 1987.

Iacocca, Lee. *Where Have All the Leaders Gone?* New York: Scribner, 2007.

Isaacson, Walter. *Benjamin Franklin: An American Life*. New York: Simon & Schuster, 2003.

Ishikawa, Kaoru. *What Is Total Quality Control? The Japanese Way*. Upper Saddle River: Prentice-Hall, Business Classics reprint, 1985.

James Madison: Architect of the Constitution and the Bill of Rights. Montpelier, Virginia: Office of the Curator, Education Department and the Constitution Center, 2004-2008. [No author listed.]

Jefferson, Thomas. *Autobiography of Thomas Jefferson*. New York: Capricorn Books, Putnam, 1959.

Johnson, Herbert. *John Jay 1745-1829*. Albany: New York State American Revolution Bicentennial Commission, 1976.

Juran, Joseph M. *Juran on Planning for Quality*. New York: Free Press, 1988.

———. and A. Blanton Godfrey. *Juran's Quality Handbook*. Milwaukee: ASQ Quality Press, Fifth Edition, 1999.

Kaplan, Robert and David Norton. *The Balanced Scorecard: Translating Strategy into Action*. Boston: Harvard Business School Press, 1996.

Ketcham, Ralph. *James Madison: A Biography*. Charlottesville: University of Virginia Press, 1990.

———. ed. *The Anti-Federalist Papers and the Constitutional Convention Debates*. New York: Signet Classic, 2003.

———. ed. *Selected Writings of James Madison*. Indianapolis: Hackett Publishing Company, 2006.

King, Bob. *Hoshin Planning: The Development Approach*. Methuen, Massachusetts: GOAL/QPC 1989.

Koch, Adrienne, ed. *Notes of Debates in the Federal Convention of 1787 Reported by James Madison*. New York: W.W. Norton & Co., 1987.

Kopeikina, Luda. *The Right Decision Every Time: How to Reach Perfect Clarity on Tough Decisions*. Upper Saddle River, New Jersey: Pearson Prentice Hall, 2005.

Kranz, Gene. *Failure is Not an Option*. New York: Simon & Schuster, 2000.

Labunski, Richard. *James Madison and the Struggle for the Bill of Rights*. New York: Oxford University Press, 2006.

Langguth, A. J. *Union 1812: The Americans who Fought the Second War of Independence*. New York: Simon & Schuster, 2006.

Leibiger, Stuart. *Founding Friendship: George Washington, James Madison, and the Creation of the American Republic*. Charlottesville: University Press of Virginia, 1999.

Lengel, Edward. *General George Washington: A Military Life*. Prince Frederick, Maryland: Recorded Books Production, Random House Audio Publishing Group. [No year listed.]

Levy, Andrew. *The First Emancipator: Slavery, Religion, and the Quiet Revolution of Robert Carter*. New York: Random House, 2005.

Levy, Leonard. *Origins of the Bill of Rights*. New Haven: Yale University Press, 2001.

Malcolm Baldrige National Quality Award. http://www.quality.nist.gov

McCoy, Drew. *The Last of the Fathers: James Madison and the Republican Legacy*. New York: Cambridge University Press, 1989.

McCullough, David. *John Adams*. New York: Simon & Schuster, 2001.

Man, Anthony "Alan Levine resigns as president of North Broward Hospital District," http://www.Sun-Sentinal.com, (January 9, 2008).

Mattern, David, ed. *James Madison's "Advice to My Country,"* Charlottesville: University of Virginia Press, 1997.

Padover, Saul. *The Living US. Constitution*. New York: Mentor Book, New American Library, 1953.

Peden, William, ed. *Notes on the State of Virginia by Thomas Jefferson*. Chapel Hill: University of North Carolina Press, 1982.

Postman, Neil. *Building a Bridge to the 18th Century: How the Past Can Improve Our Future*. New York: Vintage Books, Random House, 2000.

President John Kennedy's Special Message to the Congress on Urgent National Needs. http://millercenter.org/scripps/archive/speeches/detail/3368, May 25, 1961.

Quotations of George Washington. Bedford, Massachusetts: Applewood Books, 2003. [No editor listed.]

Rakove, Jack. *James Madison and the Creation of the American Republic*. New York: Pearson Longman, 2007.

Randall, Willard Sterne. *Thomas Jefferson: A Life*. New York: Harper Perennial, 1993.

Rutland, Robert Allen. *The Birth of the Bill of Rights 1776 – 1791*. New York: Collier Books, 1962.

——. *James Madison: The Founding Father*. Columbia: Missouri University Press, 1987.

Schermerhorn, John R., James G. Hunt, and Richard N. Osborn, Jr. *Managing Organizational Behavior*. New York: John Wiley & Sons, 1991.

Schiff, Stacy. *Great Improvisation: Franklin, France, and the Birth of America*. New York: Random House Audio Publishing Group. [No date listed.]

Scott, Mark. "How Alan Levine transformed the culture at Broward Health by developing strong bonds with his employees," *Smart Business Broward/Palm Beach*, http://www.sbnonline.com, (January 2008).

Smith, Richard Norton. *Patriarch: George Washington and the New American Nation*. Boston: Houghton Mifflin Company, 1993.

Solberg, Winton, ed. *The Federal Convention and the Formation of the Union of the American States*. New York: Liberal Arts Press, 1958.

Special Independence National Park Archives Services Bicentennial Constitutional Convention Day Book Research Project Work Files. Philadelphia: U.S. Park Service, 1987. [No editor listed.]

Sprier, Scott, Mary Fontaine, and Ruth Malloy. "Leadership Run Amok: The Destructive Potential of Overachievers," *Harvard Business Review*, (June 2006).

Stahr, Walter. *John Jay*. New York: Hambledon and London, 2005.

Staloff, Darren. *Hamilton, Adams, Jefferson: The Politics of Enlightenment and the American Founding*. New York: Hill and Wang, Farrar, Straus and Giroux, 2005.

Staton-Reinstein, Rebecca. "Engineering a Potent Business Strategy," *In Focus Magazine*, (January/February 2005) pp. 36-37.

——. "Learn from History: Successful leaders are students," Leadership Excellence, XXV, No. 11, (November 2008) p. 14.

——. *Success Planning: A 'How-To' Guide for Strategic Planning*. North Miami Beach: TobsusPress, 2003.

Stewart, David O. *The Summer of 1787: The Men Who Invented the Constitution*. New York: Simon & Schuster, 2007.

The Spark of Independence, New York: History Book Club, 1997. [No editor listed.]

Trapps, Tynisa. "Power Players Poised for Action," *South Florida Business Journal*, XXVIII (23) (January 4-8, 2008), p.11.

Tuckman, B.W. "Developmental sequence in small groups," *Psychological Bulletin*, 63(6), (1965), 384-399.

U.S. Constitution Online. http://www.usconstitution.net

Vidal, Gore. *Inventing a Nation: Washington, Adams, Jefferson*. New Haven: Yale University Press, 2003.

Vile, John. *The Constitutional Convention of 1787: A Comprehensive Encyclopedia of America's Founding*. Santa Barbara: ABC CLIO 2005, 2 volumes.

Wagner, Rodd, and James Harter. *12: The Elements of Great Managing*. New York: Gallup Press, 2007.

Washington, George. *The Journal of Major George Washington*. Williamsburg: Colonial Williamsburg Foundation, 1959.

Wiencek, Henry. *An Imperfect God: George Washington, His Slaves, and the Creation of America*. New York: Farrar, Straus and Giroux, 2003.

Wills, Garry. *James Madison*. New York: Times Books, John Holt and Company, 2002.

———. *Negro President: Jefferson and the Slave Power*. Boston: Houghton Mifflin Company, 2003.

Withey, Lynne. *Dearest Friend: A Life of Abigail Adams*. New York: Touchstone Simon & Schuster, 2002.

Wood, Gordon. *The Americanization of Benjamin Franklin*. New York: Penguin Books, 2004.

———. *Revolutionary Characters: What Made the Founders Different*. New York: Penguin Press, 2006

Disclaimer:
The author has taken all reasonable steps to ensure the accuracy of the information contained in this book. However, we can give no warranty regarding the accuracy or completeness of the content contained in this book. Hence, we accept no liability for any losses or damages (whether direct, indirect, special, consequential or otherwise) arising out of errors or omissions contained in this book.

Index

A

Adams, John 2, 17, 57, 166, 195, 223, 224, 227, 234, 243, 246, 249, 251, 252, 253

B

Baldanza, B. Ben 10, 54, 55, 62, 131, 182, 211, 212, 236
Bank of America 11, 87, 184
Broward Health 11, 76, 77, 79, 80, 81, 225, 226, 244, 251
  North Broward Hospital District 77, 226, 250
Brown, David L. 10, 150, 151, 152, 153, 154, 222, 230, 244

C

Caron, Tony 11, 29, 30, 37, 140, 141, 143, 144, 145, 146, 160, 161, 179
Carter III, Robert 125, 126, 127, 132, 229, 249
Clinton, Governor George 12, 19, 32, 49, 137, 190
CNL Bank 12, 193, 216
Coral Gables, Florida 10, 150

D

Darden Restaurants 11, 96, 183

F

Florida Shores Bank 11, 31, 88, 89
Franklin, Benjamin 19, 20, 95, 127, 128, 131, 132, 135, 154, 176, 189, 212, 213, 216, 223, 229, 230, 236, 246, 247, 251, 253

G

Gibraltar Private Bank and Trust 11, 28, 29, 30, 31, 33, 138, 139, 140, 141, 142, 143, 144, 146, 147, 160, 176, 178, 179, 182, 221

H

Hamilton, Alexander 2, 17, 19, 20, 47, 56, 66, 67, 95, 112, 122, 136, 137, 138, 147, 154, 158, 159, 162, 179, 180, 181, 182, 190, 206, 207, 213, 223, 230, 233, 244, 251

Hammerschmidt, Michael 150, 231

Hanbury II, George 10, 39, 43, 44, 45, 46, 47, 48, 49, 52, 65, 70, 71, 75

Hayworth, Steven D. 11, 28, 29, 30, 37, 138, 140, 141, 142, 143, 144, 145, 146, 147, 160, 178, 182, 223

Henry, Patrick 17, 19, 32, 137, 138, 158, 190

Hickman, Steven D. 11, 31, 37, 88, 89

Howe, Michael 11, 53, 54, 60, 61, 62, 67, 99, 100, 147, 148, 216, 217, 222, 224

J

Jay, John 136, 154, 158, 223, 248, 251

Jefferson, Thomas 10, 14, 15, 19, 39, 43, 47, 51, 56, 57, 66, 67, 69, 98, 105, 112, 120, 123, 125, 155, 159, 167, 176, 181, 182, 213, 222, 223, 224, 227, 237, 243, 244, 245, 246, 248, 250, 251, 252, 253

K

Kopeikina, Luda 11, 106, 110, 128, 171, 172, 173, 174, 227, 229, 232, 248

L

Levine, Alan 11, 76, 77, 78, 79, 80, 225, 226, 250, 251

M

Madison, James 1, 3, 4, 5, 6, 14, 15, 16, 17, 18, 19, 20, 22, 23, 27, 34, 38, 46, 47, 48, 49, 51, 83, 84, 85, 91, 112, 122, 123, 124, 125, 127, 128, 136, 137, 138, 147, 154, 155, 156, 157, 158, 159, 160, 161, 162, 163, 172, 174, 179, 180, 181, 182, 190, 191, 200, 201, 202, 206, 207, 212, 213, 221, 222, 223, 226, 228, 230, 231, 233, 237, 240, 243, 247, 248, 249, 250, 253

Jemmy 5, 14, 15, 16, 17, 221

Madison Factor 154, 158, 160, 161, 162, 163, 182, 200

Mason, George 112, 120, 125, 129, 137, 176, 190, 229, 244

MinuteClinic 11, 53, 54, 61, 62, 99, 147, 216, 217, 222

CVS Caremark 53

Morris, Gouverneur 69, 95, 112, 116, 154, 169, 223, 224, 243

N

Novak, Edward 11, 87, 88, 184, 185

Nova Southeastern University 39, 43, 48, 65

Novelty Manufacturing 13, 34, 36, 37, 222

Noventra Corporation 11, 106, 171

O

Oakland Park, Florida 12, 52, 63, 64, 200

Otis, Clarence 11, 96, 97, 183

P

PBSJ Corporation 13, 41, 42, 60, 71, 72, 73, 84, 133, 148, 149, 214

Perles, Dick 2, 5

Putnam, Howard 12, 40, 41, 58, 85, 170, 248

R

Randolph, Governor Edmund 14, 15, 16, 17, 22, 25, 28, 34, 83, 84, 85, 156, 159, 190, 229

Rees, Evan 4, 12, 99, 193, 194, 216

Ryder System 12, 59, 98, 104, 131, 135, 137, 149, 170, 194, 197, 198, 215

S

Shalala, Donna 12, 49, 50, 51, 52

Sherman, Roger 95, 115, 131

Smith, William 15

Sonesta International Hotels Corporation 12, 185, 186, 213

Sonnabend, Stephanie 12, 185, 186, 213

Southwest Airlines 12, 40, 41, 58, 85, 175

Spirit Airlines 10, 55, 62, 131, 182, 211, 212, 236

Stunson, John 12, 51, 52, 63, 64, 200, 201

Swienton, Gregory 4, 12, 59, 98, 104, 131, 135, 137, 149, 170, 194, 195, 196, 197, 198, 215, 229

T

Tansey, Stephen 12, 32, 37, 161, 162, 198, 199, 200

U

University of Miami 12, 49

W

Washington, George 9, 14, 15, 17, 18, 19, 20, 23, 27, 34, 60, 63, 65, 66, 67, 104, 110, 112, 115, 123, 127, 138, 154, 155, 156, 159, 160, 162, 166, 173, 180, 181, 182, 188, 205, 206, 207, 218, 221, 224,

227, 229, 231, 232, 234, 235, 237, 239, 243, 245, 246, 247, 249, 250, 251, 252, 253

Winger, Timothy 13, 36, 37

Y

York Container Company 13, 31-32, 163-164, 200-201, 223

Z

Zumwalt III, John 4, 13, 41, 42, 60, 69, 71, 72, 73, 85, 133, 148, 149, 214, 215, 236

Improve your meetings with dynamic Keynotes Delivered by Rebecca Staton-Reinstein

Interactive, Interesting, Innovative, Invaluable, Informative, Inspirational

Developing Strategic Leadership

Dr. Rebecca Staton-Reinstein brings you proven, practical leadership and management practices based on her many years of experience from first line manager to executive in the public, private, and non-profit sectors. She brings you insights from research with today's successful leaders and on the U.S. founding fathers. No fads, no buzz words, no management theory de jour. These are approaches that work in today's work place with today's workforce.

- Are your managers creating a stable, productive environment or are they always fighting fires?
- Are you getting the bottom-line results you want with your current approaches?
- Do you know how to unleash the power of your vision and mission?
- Do you have fully-engaged employees?

If not, contact Rebecca today for action-producing Keynotes.

Keynote Addresses

- **Conventional Wisdom**
  How your leaders and managers can apply the successful strategies of contemporary leaders, the founding fathers, and Constitutional framers

- **Stop fighting fires and get outrageous improvement**
  How strategic leadership and planning can improve your bottom line

- **What do you mean, a paycheck isn't a motivator?**
  How you can engage employees to get the results you want consistently

- **Are you the next Thomas Jefferson?**
  For college audiences: How you can fulfill your own potential with tips from the founding fathers about their college days

Advantage Leadership
Lifelong Learning for Leadership

Advantage Leadership, Inc.
663 NE 167th Street, Suite 1015,
North Miami Beach, FL 33162, USA
Tel: 305-652-3466
http://www.AdvantageLeadership.com